The Unwelcome Stranger

The Unwelcome Stranger

Valerie Cullers

The Unwelcome Stranger

This book is a work of fiction. Named locations are used fictitiously, and characters and incidents are the product of the author's imagination. Any resemblance to actual events or places or persons, living or dead, is entirely coincidental.

Published by
Lighthouse Christian Publishing
SAN 257-4330
5531 Dufferin Drive
Savage, Minnesota, 55378
United States of America

www.lighthousechristianpublishing.com

Ticinium
Verona
Genua
Cremona
Ligurian Sea
Ravenna
Italia
Adriatic Sea
Roma
Pompeii
Tyrrhenian Sea
Brundesium
Ionian Sea
Syracusae
North Africa
Carthage

Chapter One

June 312 A.D.

The air was fetid in the room. Livia had opened the curtains earlier to let some light in and now a cool breeze had begun to blow in from the sea. Her husband, Stephanas, lay in bed, his breathing labored. These last few days, he had been unable to rise from the bed and had lain there falling in and out of a fitful sleep. Every so often, Livia took a damp cloth and wiped the perspiration off his skin to help keep him clean and cool. He hadn't eaten in over a week and she could barely get him to take a sip of water this morning.

She looked at him lovingly. The handsome man she had married was hard to recognize. She could see every rib in his chest as it rose and fell with his labored breathing. In the beginning, when he began to lose weight, they took him to several physicians to see what could be done. Initially, they gave him tonics and potions to increase his appetite, but nothing had helped. Finally, the physicians diagnosed his problem as "the wasting disease."

Eventually, they said there wasn't much more that could be done. They had given him strong herbs to help with the pain, but in the end, even they hadn't helped much. Stephanas had endured the loss of his strength over the last two years, and this past week had finally endured his final loss, that of being able to get out of bed and walk.

Stephanas just lay there and barely opened his eyes. He knew the end was near and felt sorely the regret of leaving his beloved wife. They had been married only five short years. He had expected to spend many more years together with her, but sadly it was not to be. He was leaving her a widow at the age of twenty. Their life now seemed like it had been a fleeting dream together. As he thought of it, he smiled, for he now cherished every moment he had been able to spend in her presence.

His final concerns had been for her welfare. He had spoken with his father, Junius, about them. Junius had assured him that he would love and care for her as he would his own daughter. He had promised him he would see to her welfare when he was gone.

Stephanas knew he could trust his father, for he was a kind and loving man who kept his word. He had assured Stephanas that when the time came, he would find a suitable husband for her. He promised that he wouldn't force her to marry against her will. Stephanas would have to content himself with this, knowing he had left his wife in good hands.

Livia had been a lovely girl and had grown into a beautiful woman. He never tired of looking at her face. Her green almond-shaped eyes had captured him from the moment he first looked upon her. She had come to the estate with Julia, his mother's cousin, when his mother had first taken ill. Livia was Julia's only daughter and had come to help her care for his mother. During that year, he had become more and more attached to her. When his mother died, he realized he didn't want to live without Livia. He had asked Julia for her hand in marriage and they were married within a month of his mother's death.

She had been with him ever since. As part of her dowry, she had given him a small chest of golden aurei[1]. He had not touched any of it, hoping they would use it to add to their acreage in the future. Once he knew he would not recover, he returned it to her. He wanted her to have it, should she ever need it. Perhaps it would become her dowry again in the future. It pained him to even think of her marrying another.

Regretfully, there would be no heir of his to inherit his share of his father's estate. They had both hoped for children, but they had never come. Every month he watched her disappointed face when her monthly flow started. He had tried to assure her that her love was all that he needed, but she had never truly believed it. His only concern was that without an heir, she would have no legal rights in the household - not that women had many rights, but an heir would guarantee her some status in the household. She would have a secure place, should his brother come home and bring a wife with him.

It didn't matter to him that his brother, Marcus, would inherit the entire estate when his father passed. He was concerned how his brother would treat Livia when he came home to live and help his father. He had resented her from the beginning. She had taken his place as his brother's confidant, and he had never forgiven her for that. He had seen little of Marcus these past five years. Shortly after they were married, he had left to work for his uncle in Ravenna. His uncle Rufus was a wealthy wine merchant who owned a large warehouse in the Caesarea district. When he was gone, his brother would be returning to help his father with the estate. His brother would resent that, too. He had

[1] Roman gold coins, each worth twenty-five denarii

become quite fond of his life in the city, and only came home on occasion to visit.

What a predicament he was leaving his wife in. This bothered him the most as he lay dying. He hadn't the energy to talk about it as he could barely open his eyes. She had been giving him sweet wine mixed with herbs and he had slept much of the last few days away. He had refused it this morning as he wanted to be conscious until the end, and spend his final hours with his wife, awake and alert. He had said farewell to his father this morning and now Junius was leaving them alone for their final hours together. He could barely speak, and he wanted her to know how much he loved her and had appreciated her loving care during his illness.

She sat there quietly, as she had for so many days. She didn't beg him to fight the disease and not leave her as she had done in the beginning. It was too late for that now. He had fought the disease, but in the end, it had been stronger than he was. They both knew that it wouldn't be long now.

He opened his eyes and looked at her. She noticed it and asked if she could do anything for him. He shook his head weakly and just squeezed her hand. He opened his mouth to speak, but he could only mouth her name. He took his final breath and released it slowly. It was his final act and he was gone.

Livia sat there numbly for a few moments, and then lay down beside him in the bed. She wanted to hold him one last time before the servants came to take the body to prepare it for burial. She would call them in a few moments, but for now she wanted to embrace the man she had married and loved. She held him until the warmth began to leave his body. She kissed him goodbye one last time and looked at him. She knew she would not see him again until they met in the afterlife.

She could feel the Lord's presence in the room. It had been practically palpable these last few days. The sense of strength and peace she had felt for months became stronger. She felt totally bereft at her loss, and yet she knew without a shadow of doubt that she was not alone. It was the only thing that gave her comfort at this moment.

Slowly, she rose from the bed. She had to force herself to leave his side. Her feet felt leaden as she walked to the door. She looked back to where his body lay, and opened the door. She started to call for Claudius, their aging servant, but he was just a few feet from the door sitting on a stool. He had known Stephanas since he was a child, and was just as concerned for him as she was. She looked at him and nodded.

Tears began to stream from his eyes as he came into the room and looked at his body on the bed. He turned away towards the window. He opened the curtains fully to let the light completely in. He was trying to control his emotions as he hid his face from her for a few moments. He stood there and took a few deep breaths, then let out a long sigh. He turned and all he could say to her was, "Oh, Mistress."

Livia left to find her father-in-law, Junius, and tell him that Stephanas was gone. He looked up as she came into the room. Livia didn't have to say a word; he knew what she had to say by the look on her face. He stood up and Livia let herself fall into his arms. She started sobbing and he held her. He began to walk her back to her room. As they passed Rhea, Livia's servant since childhood, he asked her to bring Livia a glass of undiluted wine. He waited until Rhea brought it and then told Livia to drink it because it would calm her and help her to rest.

Livia lay on her bed and for the first time in months, went into a deep sleep. It was dusk when she awoke, and she realized she had slept the entire afternoon. Her stomach was growling as she got up and began to straighten her stola[2]. She moved to the bench by her dressing table. She looked into the mirror but couldn't see her face clearly.

She opened her door and was glad to see they had lit the lamps early. She walked down the hall and went straight to the kitchen. The house was quiet, and the servants were in their quarters. Whatever had been served for dinner had been put away, but she knew there would be some cheese and bread to be found. There was a full pitcher of water sitting by the sink. She poured herself a glass and drank deeply. It was refreshing, as usual, and she felt grateful for the well on their property.

She chewed the bread slowly and took small sips of water to help wash it down. She knew she must try to eat something, but she had no interest in food. If her stomach hadn't been growling, she wouldn't even bother. She hadn't eaten since this morning and had only eaten a few bites then. She had known what was coming and had been trying to prepare herself for the end.

The light from the oil lamp on the wall produced a small glow in the dark kitchen. She felt her life was like that now; there was a small light inside of her but on the outside, there was only darkness and death. She continued eating and was grateful for the silence in the room. She didn't want to talk to anyone right now; she just wanted to feel her own pain. Soon she would go back to her room and try to sleep, but she knew sleep would not come easily. There were too many emotions to feel and too many thoughts to think, and yes, too many tears to cry. And

[2] An overdress or skirt worn over the tunic of a married woman.

tonight, unlike most nights, she would not try to hold her grief in so that her husband would not hear her cry across the hall.

This night was truly different than the others, for she knew she would not see Stephanas when she awoke in the morning. She could only look forward to the time when she would see him after death; and only the Lord knew when that time would come for her. It would probably be years, she thought, as she finished eating.

She got up to go to her room and had the sense that her life would never be the same again. When Stephanas had taken his last breath, her life had changed forever. She had gotten up this morning a married woman, and was going to bed a widow. Her future seemed bleak indeed without the man she loved. She didn't want to go to sleep and wake up to her new life without him. She lay down in her bed and continued thinking about her future. It seemed like hours passed before her lids grew heavy. She was relieved when the exhaustion numbed her mind and she could not think clearly. Soon, she closed her eyes and went into a fitful, dreamless sleep.

Chapter Two

Marcus was sitting at his desk working on the accounts; he heard the commotion before he saw it. His father's servant, Prosper, had come through the door and was talking to his uncle. From the look on his face, Marcus knew that it was not good news. He knew his brother had been ill, but it had been a month since he had been home to see him. He knew he was not getting any better, but he had refused to face the fact that Stephanas might die soon.

He willed himself to rise from his chair and walked slowly to the front of the building. He didn't want to hear the news about his brother and he didn't want to have to face the decisions that would be coming from this unbidden change in his family's circumstances.

Marcus had always loved his older brother, but they had been as different as night and day. They had been especially close until soon after their mother died. Then Stephanas had wed Livia and their close friendship changed. He began to confide in her instead of him. Marcus felt bereft by the loss of his mother, and didn't know how to take the change in relationship with his brother. He blamed Livia for the distance she created between them, and he had continued to resent her these past five years.

Stephanas and he were opposites. Stephanas had loved the land and could talk for hours on the state of the crops and the health of the animals. He was very inventive and was always thinking of new ways to make the estate run better. Marcus had been interested in the estate when he was younger, but as he grew into a teenager, he began to yearn for a different life. His mind begged to be challenged and he grew bored with the daily routine of taking care of the animals and the crops. He knew he wasn't cut out to be a farmer and wanted to spend his days in a more exciting setting.

He was also at odds with his family's religion. His parents had become Christians eighteen years earlier and had left the pantheon of Roman gods behind. Even when the Edicts of Prohibition had been issued under the Emperor Diocletian[3] nine years ago, and they had been threatened with death and persecution, they had not wavered in their beliefs. They had continued to meet with the church in secret and their faith had actually grown stronger.

They had taught their sons about their beliefs since childhood. Stephanas had become an ardent follower of Christ. His faith had grown even stronger with every passing month of his sickness. When Marcus had come home to visit, his brother always shared how the Lord was helping him cope with his illness. Marcus listened attentively, and tried to encourage his brother, but he did not have the faith Stephanas had.

Marcus believed in the Lord as a child and had loved the intrigue and danger of meeting with the church when it had been outlawed by the state. The authorities had arrested the leaders of the churches and had taken over all of the church buildings in Ravenna. Instead of large gatherings, the community of believers split up to meet in smaller groups. Marcus's family joined with two others in the area and they varied the meeting place weekly. After a few years, however, the authorities in the area lost their zeal for persecuting the church. It was still against the law to meet

---

[3] First Roman Emperor to divide the Empire into a Tetrarchy. He divided the Empire into an eastern and western region. He had a senior Augustus and a subordinate Caesar rule half of each region.

together, and so the church continued to meet in secret, but the sense of danger was gone.

As the element of danger lessened, Marcus's sense of adventure did, too. His thoughts began to wander during the services. He yearned to experience life to the fullest and the thought of denying himself and living for a heavenly kingdom did not appeal to him in the least. As these ideas grew stronger in his mind; his interest in Christianity began to wane.

Marcus had enjoyed his family's monthly trips into Ravenna to get supplies. There was so much to see and so much going on. He loved the sights and smells and the bustle of activity in the market place. Ravenna even had its own place in Roman history; Julius Caesar had made it his headquarters while he awaited his promised Consulship from Pompey. When Pompey and the Senate refused to keep their promise to him, Julius Caesar marched his Thirteenth Legion into Ravenna and weighed his options. As he calculated the strength of his army and odds for a military victory, he ordered his legion to march south and make camp beside the Rubicon. When he came to meet them a few days later, he saw what he thought was a sign from the gods assuring him of victory. There on the banks of that river, he made his final decision to march on Rome. He crossed the Rubicon and within three months had conquered the entire country. In honor of his victory, Ravenna named the trade district southeast of the city, Caesarea.

Marcus dreamed of living in the city, and little did he know that his dreams would come true. Shortly after Stephanas and Livia were married, his uncle Rufus had come to the estate to visit his father. The two of them had spent the afternoon in the library privately discussing matters. After dinner they returned to the library and asked Marcus to join them. Because his uncle had no sons and three young daughters, he asked Junius if Marcus could come live with him and learn the wine business. He hoped that as he grew older, he could turn the business over to Marcus. If Marcus could find it in his heart to marry one of his daughters when the time came, so much the better. It would give Rufus the security that his family would be taken care of when he was gone.

Marcus could not believe what he had heard; the plan seemed too good to be true. His father had approved of the idea, and if Marcus wanted, he could go and live with his uncle. Marcus agreed heartily with the idea and packed his belongings that night. He left with his uncle the next morning. From that day to this, he had made his home with his uncle and had not regretted the decision once. He saw his family when they came into the city once a month. Once a year, he went home to give his father a hand with the harvest. When it was finished, he was always happy to return to his life in the city.

He had returned a month ago, specifically to visit Stephanas. His brother had been getting weaker and weaker and no longer came into the city. The day Marcus had come, Stephanas had seemed stronger and it had even given him hope that his brother would rally. Marcus had left that evening with the false hope of his brother's improvement. He refused to believe that his brother would die. It would change everything in his life, and he didn't want to entertain those thoughts.

Marcus had even made peace with Livia on his last visit home. He thanked her for her care of his brother and even told his brother how fortunate he was to have her. Stephanas had looked at him with surprise at that comment.

For years, Marcus hardly acknowledged Livia's existence and never spoke a word directly to her. Stephanas remarked that his brother really was growing up and maturing. It had been a good day for Marcus. He felt closer to his brother than he had in years. They talked of their youth and how they were both so different and how their lives had taken different directions.

Their differences really began to surface when their father had brought in a tutor. Stephanas had been bored with the scrolls and could hardly wait to get outdoors. Marcus, on the other hand, loved to learn and hear about what was happening in the empire. There were plenty of stories to hear about their history and he wanted to hear all of them. He loved to hear about the conquests and battles, politics and intrigue. The tutor found he was especially good at mathematics and could do all kinds of calculations in his head.

When Stephanas was finished with his studies, he was relieved. Marcus, on the other hand, did not want his time of learning to end. He felt a deep loss when the tutor quit coming. He went back to the fields and again longed for more intellectual stimulation. He always enjoyed working around his brother, though. His brother knew more about the crops and was always trying to teach him about them. Stephanas could lift up a clod of dirt and tell if it was good soil and what needed to be planted in it. Marcus tried to show an interest, but all he could see in the dirt was the hard physical labor it represented. Neither the dirt nor the hard physical labor appealed to him.

All of these thoughts tumbled through his mind as he slowly walked the length of the warehouse. He reached the two men and they stopped talking. He looked at Prosper and said, "Is it Stephanas?"

"Yes, I'm afraid he passed late this morning," Prosper said.

Marcus stood there stunned for a few moments. He tried to take in the fact that his brother was really gone. He began to feel the weight of grief as it began to engulf him. He took a few deep breaths to steady his emotions. His next thought was of the burden of responsibility he must now assume. His loving, kind and gentle brother was not going to take his rightful place on the family estate. What a hole that was going to leave for his father. Marcus knew his father would need him and that his life was going to change from this moment on. He could feel the resentment building inside of him. Why couldn't his brother have lived so that he could pursue the life he had wanted? He knew that he would be expected to return soon and make his home there permanently.

Was this God's idea of a cruel joke? Marcus was beginning to think so. He looked at Rufus and knew his uncle must be thinking about the changes this news would bring to him also. His uncle looked sad, just like he was, and for the same multitude of reasons.

"I need to leave, Uncle," Marcus said.

"I know, Son. We will be along tomorrow to see your family. Tell my brother we will come for the funeral and will be there by midmorning."

Marcus headed out the door. He would need to go to his uncle's stable to get his horse. It would take a few hours to ride home with Prosper. He felt his stomach tighten at the thought of having to face what was coming. Why, why did this have to happen to him?

Chapter Three

Junius Arvum lay on his bed with his eyes wide open; a multitude of thoughts running through his mind. He knew sleep would not come easily this night - there was too much to think about. He stared at the flickering lights that danced under his door from the oil lamp in the hall and went over the day's events.

This had been one of the most difficult days in his life. Earlier in the day they had lain his son's body in the family crypt. He had hoped he would be the next one laid to rest there, sharing the space with his wife's body. Instead, they had placed Stephanas in a recently carved niche this morning.

Shortly after Rufus and his family arrived, they had started the funeral ceremony. Thaumas, the elder in their small group of believers, led the prayers and singing. Junius had been comforted by the well-chosen words and they confirmed his hope that he would see his son again. Tonight, however, he was feeling the impact of his loss, and he ached for his son's presence.

News of Stephanas's death had spread quickly through the surrounding area. This afternoon many neighbors had stopped by to offer their condolences. The hours continued to crawl by as he spoke with their friends and acquaintances. When Junius closed the front door, relieved that the last guest had left, he saw Marcus sitting in an alcove of the peristyle[4]; his head in his hands. He knew once the guests were gone, his son could finally be alone. He would be able to release his pent-up emotions and finally grieve. Junius looked at him and felt his pain but said nothing. No words could replace the loss of his brother, so he walked by quietly.

---

[4] an open courtyard surrounded by a colonnade

As he walked towards the kitchen, he saw Livia. She looked exhausted from talking with so many people. She quietly excused herself and left to go to bed. He watched the servants cleaning up the kitchen, putting the leftover food away. Junius decided to go to bed also, coveting the privacy of his own bedroom and his thoughts of his son.

Stephanas had been born to the land and everything it represented. His elder son had worked with him for almost two decades. He felt at home on the land and was interested in every detail that would help it become more fruitful. He had been like an extension of his right hand from the time he was a young teenager. He seemed to relish his time outdoors and never grew tired of the work. Even when he was ill, he would help make decisions about the planting, care and harvesting of each crop they had. He especially liked the grape vines, and knew exactly how to prune each one so that it would produce more grapes the following year.

Now he was gone and Junius didn't have someone to share in the daily running of the farm. It wasn't that he didn't want Marcus to come and help him; he loved his younger son. It was just that he knew Marcus didn't want to come and work on the estate and take over for him when the time came. It wasn't that Marcus didn't know what to do; he had also helped since he was a young child. But he only helped because the work needed to be done, not because he truly loved it.

These past few years, Rufus had told him how well Marcus did with buying and selling the wine for his warehouse. Marcus had the knack for being able to tell a good wine from a truly fine one - the kind he could get hundreds of sesterces[5] a bottle for. He had actually

---

[5] A Roman Coin, 25 sesterces equal 1 denarius

increased his uncle's business because of his ability to seek out the truly exceptional wines in the surrounding regions. His reputation grew and people were bringing their wines from further and further away in order to get a better price. Another ten years and Marcus would be running the business by himself.

Rufus had sought Junius out this afternoon and spoke with him privately. He told him that he was releasing Marcus from their previous agreement. He would send Marcus back whenever Junius wanted him. Junius appreciated his brother's generosity, but it pained him to think of taking Marcus away from something he loved so much. He didn't actually need the day to day help on the land; he had several servants who had been helping him for years. He would only need Marcus's help during the harvest season.

Junius continued to think about Marcus and what would be best for him. Marcus would inherit the estate now, and with the right caretaker, could easily run the operation from town. He would need to come out every month to check on things, but that shouldn't be a problem if he wanted to manage it from a distance.

His thoughts then turned to Livia. He had promised Stephanas that he would take care of her as long as he was alive, but what would happen to her when he was gone? She had managed his home since the early part of her marriage to Stephanas and she was a vital part of it. She brought a warmth and caring to all she did for them. She managed their resources wisely and worked well with the servants. What would happen to her when he was gone and Marcus brought his wife into the home to claim his inheritance? Would Livia be relegated to little more than a hired servant? He hated the thought and wondered what he could do to prevent that from happening.

He began asking the Lord to show him what to do about the problem. What should he do to protect this young woman from what was to come? He could try to find a husband for her, but the thought of losing her was more than he could bear right now. She had become like a daughter to him, and he knew he would be bereft if she left also.

As the minutes went by, an idea began to form in his mind. Within a short time, he felt he had a solution to his concerns. The only problem was that Marcus was not going to like it...no, Marcus would not like it one single bit. With that thought in mind, Junius smiled to himself, relaxed and went to sleep.

Chapter Four

Marcus slapped the reins on the horse's flanks. His anger knew no bounds at the moment. He couldn't believe what his father had just told him. He had come home, mourning his brother's death and wanting to share this time of grief with his father. He had come down to breakfast this morning, hoping to talk to his father about the ceremony yesterday and how his brother's life had been honored by so many guests. He also needed to talk to him about what he wanted him to do now. Instead what did he get? The morning after his brother's burial, even though his father's hand hadn't touched him, he felt as if he had been slapped in the face.

Marcus had been prepared to help his father, and return to the villa as soon as necessary. He had been mentally preparing himself for the inevitable, that of taking his brother's place in the care and management of the estate. He knew the entire estate would be left to him someday and that he must begin to assume responsibility for it now that Stephanas was gone. It was a huge sacrifice for him, but he knew he must make it for his father's sake. However, this was too much!

Before he could even start a conversation, his father had informed him that he had decided to leave the estate to both he and Livia. He said he was not going to leave her without a home in which she had some ownership in. He wanted her to have equal rights in the property so that when the time came, she would have some status in the home. He didn't want her living like a servant in the house when Marcus decided to take a wife. What an insult! Did his father think he would throw her out when he got married? Why would his father do this to him?

He rode further with his anger coming in waves. He couldn't make the horse go fast enough to suit him. If only he could strike the ground with his fists the same way the horse's hooves were pounding the ground. That's what he felt like, he wanted to beat on something, anything to get the rage out. He had never been angrier or more insulted in his entire life!

As he neared Ravenna, he stopped to let the horse drink and to calm himself before he returned to his uncle's house. He would need to have the stable boy rub the horse down when he returned, as it was dripping with sweat. He had not meant to make the horse run so fast, but it was the only way Marcus could get his anger out. He had to admit he felt better even if he didn't have a solution for his problem. He didn't want to share the estate with his sister-in-law. He could foresee all kinds of problems this arrangement would bring in the future.

If she married again, would another man come into the house and try to assume his brother's role? Would he and some other man have to work together in running the estate? It seemed so wrong to have to share the responsibility with a stranger he had never met! And then it hit him, he realized what his father had intended with this decision.

How could he have been so blind? His father wanted him to marry Livia at some point in the future! That was his intent. Marcus's anger dissipated and he felt defeated. Instead of asking him to marry Livia outright, his father had squarely placed the decision before him. He didn't have to marry her, but if he didn't, he would have to share the estate with another.

It's not that he didn't care for Livia; he did, but he saw her as a sister, not as the woman he wanted to marry. Yes, she had been perfect for his brother; they both had lived a contented life on the farm. They had seemed happy enough in their agrarian environment, and in a way, he had been envious of them. How could they live so far from everything that was happening and handle the monotony of their existence? Yes, he had envied them their contentment, but he had not wanted it for himself.

And now, nothing would ever be the same again. At the moment he didn't want to think of anything; his home, the estate, Livia, his father, any of it. As he sat by the stream, his grief and frustration spilled out and tears came to his eyes. Why, why must he be faced with this decision? Not only was it not fair; it was not right. His father knew him, and knew he would never be happy living in the country. and now he was faced with another choice he did not want to make.

Well, he wouldn't do it; at least not now. No one could make him and if he had to marry her, it could wait several years while he lived the life he wanted to. "So there, take that, my scheming father!" As Marcus voiced those thoughts, he felt no better. Just as he was sitting at the stream situated between town and the country estate, he felt his life was hanging between those same two places. He didn't belong to either now and he didn't know what he was going to do about it.

Marcus got back on his horse and continued riding into town. This time he rode slower, continually thinking about his future. The thought of living on the farm with Livia was repugnant to him. Perhaps he could live in town and have the farm run by a manager, when the time came. He dismissed the thought for the moment. His grief had drained him emotionally and this new development had tired him mentally. By the time he got to the stable, his emotions were spent and he felt completely demoralized.

He left the horse with the stable boy and walked down the street to the warehouse. His uncle was talking with a customer and the look on his face told him he was surprised to see him. Marcus walked to the far end of the building and turned his back to them; staring intently at a row of wine barrels. A few moments later he heard his uncle's footsteps approach.

"Marcus, what are you doing here? I thought you would at least stay with your father for a few more days," his uncle said.

Marcus turned towards him. His face reflected the anguish he was feeling. He wondered about how much he should tell his uncle. He decided to tell him everything - it would all come out sooner or later anyway. He took a deep breath and began, "I walked down to breakfast this morning, intent on telling my father that I would help him with whatever he needed. Before I got a word out, he told me that he had decided to leave Stephanas's share of the estate to Livia. I would not own the property outright, but would have to share ownership with her. I was so angry with him that I got up and left for town."

His uncle looked at him for a few moments, his face filled with compassion. He shook his head and began to chuckle, "Why that sly fox! I didn't know he had it in him."

Marcus looked at him, not seeing the humor in the whole situation, "So you guessed immediately what he was after?"

His uncle chuckled. "It's obvious, Marcus. He doesn't want to marry Livia off to another man. He's grown so attached to her that he wants to keep her in the family."

Up to this point, Marcus had not considered his father's feelings. The man had first lost his wife and now his son. He probably could not face the thought of another loss at the moment. "It does make sense when you look at it from his perspective. I just thought he was trying to run my life from beyond the grave. He's had complete control my whole life and I was hoping for a little independence when he passed," Marcus admitted grudgingly.

"You know you are like a son to me," Rufus began, "and I would love for you to continue your work here. As you know, I had wanted you to be my heir and take over my business when the time came. Yesterday, I told Junius that I was releasing you both from our agreement. You're his son, and I want you to do whatever he needs you to do."

Marcus had seen them both go into the library and talk. He thought his uncle would say something along those lines to his father. He appreciated his uncle's generosity, considering all of the time he had spent training him. "I have no desire to go back there, and I have no desire to marry Livia," he spat out bitterly. The words sounded cold and unfeeling, but Marcus didn't care.

"Your father knows that," Rufus said. "He doesn't need you right now and he doesn't want to take you away from here. He even spoke of you hiring a manager for the estate when the time came."

Marcus was surprised at his father's thoughtfulness. In his anger he had not let his father continue the conversation. He had just erupted and stormed out of the dining room. With this new information there was a lot to think about. Now, there was the possibility of running the wine business in town and managing the estate in the country. The cost of having both would be to cooperate with his father and take Livia for his wife. Perhaps his options were not so bad after all. "So, what do I do for now?" he asked quietly.

"Continue to work here for me. Your father and I will work out a schedule that allows you to go back and forth and learn what you need to in order to run the estate. You will need to learn it all, especially if you are going to hire a manager in the future. Now son, think about what your father is asking and see if you can find it in your heart to marry the woman when the time comes. It really doesn't seem too much to ask, considering all you have to gain," Rufus said.

"When you say it that way, it doesn't seem so bad after all," Marcus replied. He realized he was being handed more than he could have dreamed of. He felt ashamed of his immediate reaction and the way he had stormed out of his father's house. "I guess I owe my father an apology," he said.

"Yes, you do, and you'll get your chance sooner than you think. He is going to come into town this week and we are going to discuss which months will be best for you to go out to the farm and learn the business there," Rufus explained.

Marcus felt himself bristle inside. His life was being decided for him and he had no part in the decisions, as usual. At twenty, he wanted to be considered a man and have a say in his future. He let the feeling pass before he spoke and he chose his words carefully. He did not want to appear ungrateful for the opportunity that was being set before him. "What months do you think that will be, Uncle?" he asked.

"Probably one or two in the spring so you can learn the planting cycle and one or two in the fall so that you are there for the harvest. Your father knows that you are familiar with how he does things, but he wants to train you like he did your brother, so that you will really understand the operation," Rufus replied.

Marcus began to feel overwhelmed by the thought of so much responsibility in the future. He had never considered the thought that he might have to manage two businesses. He sat down on the nearest stool. He loved a challenge, but this seemed so overwhelming. "Do you think I can do it all?" he asked his uncle.

His uncle came over to him and slapped him on the back. "Of course, I do; we're both counting on you." His uncle laughed heartily

Marcus looked up at him, his emotions vying for his attention. He had never felt so many competing emotions all at once, and he didn't want to give in to any of them. He looked at his uncle, "I think I need some time to think about it all," he said.

"Go, take all the time you need. I don't need you here today," Rufus said.

Marcus stood and turned to go. He walked a few steps and turned back to his uncle.

"Thank you, Uncle Rufus. I don't know what I would do without you. You seem to understand me so much better than my father does."

Rufus looked at him. "He understands you, too, Marcus, and he wants to do what's best for you. I believe he wants to do what's best for all of us."

Marcus could see that now. As his father, he had every right to order him to return home and help on the estate. He even had the right to tell him to marry Livia. He was not doing that. He was trying to consider everyone's needs; his son's, his brother's and his daughter-in-law's. He had obviously thought this out and he was trying to find the best solution for all of them. "You're right, as usual, Uncle," Marcus replied.

He turned to go, thoughts whirling in his brain. He needed to think, and he did it best at a quiet spot overlooking the Adriatic. He needed to get his emotions under control also.

Rufus watched him walk out of the warehouse. He was proud of his older brother, and how they had worked together to plan this young man's future. Marcus was intelligent, but he had a lot of growing up to do. He especially needed to learn how to control his emotions. He walked to the door of the warehouse and continued to watch as Marcus walked up the street towards the sea. "He just needs time to get used to the idea," he thought to himself.

Chapter Five

August 312 AD

Livia looked out the window in the kitchen. Breakfast was over and the dishes were clean, so she took a few moments to savor the view. She loved the beauty of the land and how it gave its bounty to them each fall. She should be looking forward to the harvest season, but with the events of this summer, she couldn't think past today.

She had no sense of peace as she looked on the fields. All Italia was bracing for war, but no one knew when it would come. Constantine, the Caesar who ruled Britannia and Gaul, had invaded the northern part of Italia this summer. He and his army were camped at Mediolanum[6], and everyone knew that eventually he would march on Rome. All of the cities, including Ravenna, were making plans should he and his army come their way. That was all everyone seemed to talk about at the market; the imminent danger of the invading army.

Livia knew she should care about all that was happening around her, and yet she felt disconnected from it all. She had lost Stephanas and that is all that really mattered to her. As far as she was concerned, her life was over; she only went through the motions each day because she had to. She looked forward to each night, when she could go to bed and let her grief out privately.

It had been two months since Stephanas had passed, and yet she still couldn't get used to how alone she felt. Each day she dwelt on past memories of him. She didn't want to think of the future because the future she had

[6] Modern day Milan, Italy

planned with him would never come to pass. The children she would have liked to have had with him didn't exist; instead there was just a deep emptiness inside of her. Her hope of a life together with him had died when he died, and it had been buried with him inside the family crypt this summer.

She knew all widows must feel like this; she just hadn't been prepared to feel this way at twenty. As she was looking out at the vineyard, she heard a commotion behind her. She turned and saw Rhea walking quickly towards her.

"Livia, come quickly," Rhea called.

She followed her towards the atrium[7]. She heard the sound of men's voices and they were unfamiliar to her. As she entered the atrium, she froze at the scene in front of her. She had hoped to never see soldiers in her home again after her previous experience with them. The memories flooded her mind as she stood there.

The family's peristyle villa[8] was situated fifteen miles north of Ravenna. Their land was on both sides of the main coastal road - the Via Popillia Annia. The road had been built four hundred years earlier in order to connect Ariminum[9], further south on the coast of the Adriatic, to Aquileia in the north of Italia. The family was used to seeing all sorts of travelers and had seen soldiers many times, but their last experience with them had been devastating.

Six years ago, while Stephanas's mother lay ill, the Emperor Galerius was marching his Illyrian army down the coast of Italia on his way to Rome. Emperor Galerius was

---

[7] The main reception area or salon in a Roman home

[8] A farmstead built around a courtyard with a colonnade portico on all sides

[9] Modern day Rimini, Italy

feared by all the citizens of the empire, but he was especially feared by Christians because of his hatred of their religion.

The previous Emperor, Diocletian, had signed edicts prohibiting the practice of Christianity four years earlier. However, most Christians believed that the reason they were drawn up was because Galerius had poisoned Diocletian's mind with false accusations about them. Galerius had spent the winter of 302 at Diocletian's palace and the following spring the first edict came out.

Two years after the edict was signed, Diocletian retired and Galerius became the Emperor of the eastern half of the Roman empire. To the Christians he became known as "The Beast," because of his relentless persecution of the church. The Christians on this side of the Adriatic had heard many a story of his ruthlessness when dealing with their brothers in the east.

There was one man who wasn't afraid of him, though. His name was Maxentius; he was the son of the previous Emperor of the western half of the Roman empire, Maximian. He rebelled against Galerius and assumed the title of Caesar in Rome, and began governing Italia and the countries of northern Africa.

Galerius was determined to stamp out this rebellion with the help of his Illyrian army. While en route to Rome, Galerius infuriated the Italian populace by requisitioning supplies for his army without payment in return. The Arvum family had experienced this personally when the supply sergeant showed up at their door and demanded provisions. He took most of their herd of sheep, along with their supply of grain, oil and wine. The loss had cost the family dearly and came at a difficult time. It had taken the family several years to recover from their losses.

As these thoughts were going through Livia's mind, she took a deep breath to try to regain her composure and prayed a silent prayer for help. She walked forward and began to assess the situation. Two soldiers were standing in the atrium; one was carrying the body of a man dressed in a toga. On further inspection, she noticed that the toga had a purple stripe down the side - evidence that he was a high government official.

"Mistress," the older soldier said. "Your sheep were in the road as we turned the corner. The Legate's chariot could not stop in time and it overturned. He's breathing but he's not conscious."

Livia sensed danger from the first moment she saw the soldiers. If the Arvum's sheep were in the road and had caused this accident, it did not bode well for them. "Follow me," she said. She led them to Stephanas's room and had them place his body on the bed. She turned to Rhea who had been following behind the soldiers, "Bring me a bowl of warm water, soap and towels. Please send one of the servants to find Junius. Ask him to send for the physician."

As soon as Rhea returned with the water and soap, Livia began to clean the Legate's body. They carefully removed his toga and then his tunic. She began to wash the dirt off his arms and legs. She placed oil on all of the scrapes and bandaged those that needed covered. The soldiers held him in a sitting position while she bathed his back and wiped the dirt from his hair. She saw a large bruise on the back of his head where he must have landed. When they laid him back down, she finally bathed his face. He was still breathing, thank God, and perhaps he would live. Otherwise, who knows what would happen to them.

When she finished bathing him, the soldiers helped put a clean tunic on him. The cloth was rough compared to the quality of the toga they had taken off. She placed a light blanket over him to keep him warm. She could feel the soldiers watch her every move and it made her nervous. Every now and then, she wiped the sweat off his face with a wet cloth. It probably didn't help anything, but it gave her something to do. She noticed his ashen face had gained some color since they brought him in. "Live, live," she silently spoke to him in her mind, willing him to awake.

"Who is this man?" she asked, as she looked from one soldier to the other.

"He is Lucius Marius, a Senatorial Legate. He was returning to his home in Ravenna after being in Mediolanum on the Senate's business," the older soldier replied.

She could feel the fear rising in her throat. She began to taste her own bile and it made her want to wretch. Everyone knew who Lucius Marius was; he was from the most distinguished family in Ravenna. His father was a senator in Rome and Lucius had obtained the office of Legate because of his father's connections. His family had descended from the legendary General Marius who had completely restructured the Roman army. General Marius had also been key in Ravenna's maritime development. To honor him, Ravenna had placed a marble statue of him in its forum[10]. If this man died, they could be imprisoned and their property confiscated. If he lived, but was severely injured, there could still be serious consequences for them.

Time seemed to slow down. She watched Lucius's chest rise and fall as they waited for the physician. It seemed like hours passed until she heard his footsteps approach the bedroom door. Their physician, Hector, came in with a worried look on his face. He knew there was

---

[10] The public square of ancient Roman cities

danger here for him also, depending on how the patient fared. He asked the soldiers to describe the accident again and how the patient had landed on the ground. With that information, he began evaluating his new patient.

He opened his eyelids and looked into his pupils. He looked at his head in the front and back to see his wounds. He winced as he saw the large bruise on the back of his head where he had hit the ground. He felt his stomach area and rolled him over gently to look at his back. He felt each arm and leg to make sure there were no broken bones.

He turned and spoke to the soldiers and Livia, "As you saw, it looks like the main injury is to his head, the arms and legs and the rest of his body appear to be without serious injury. A fall like that can kill a person or cause great damage to the brain. We are fortunate he did not break his neck. We will only be able to ascertain the extent of his injuries when and if he wakes up. I will remain here with him until we know something further."

The blood drained from Livia's face as she sat down in the chair beside the bed. This was the very same chair she had sat in to nurse Stephanas, and now there was another man in his room, possibly dying also. She had thought that her husband's death was the worst thing that could happen to her; but this, this could turn out to be much worse. "Lord," she prayed silently, "help this man to live and give me the strength to do whatever I need to do."

She turned to the soldiers, "Sirs, would you like some food or refreshment of some sort? Please let us offer you a place to rest as we wait for the Legate to recover."

They looked at each other pondering the offer. They were his personal guard, and would only leave him if they thought he was safe. They would have to answer to his father if any harm came to him and there was an element of fear in their eyes also. “Yes, we will take something to drink and eat,” the older of the two said. “He is safe, for now, and who knows how long we will be here.”

They followed her to the kitchen. She felt their eyes boring into her back as she walked. She tried to walk normally and show no sign of the fear she felt. The smell of warm bread was still lingering in the kitchen from this morning when it came out of the oven. She broke a loaf in two and gave them each half. She set cheese and fruit before them and poured a glass of water for each one. They said little as they ate and when they had finished, followed her back to the room in silence.

The scene had not changed since they had left it a half an hour before. Livia left them to make sure there were rooms prepared for the soldiers to sleep in tonight. Thankfully, she saw that Rhea had already taken care of it and everything was in readiness. She returned to the kitchen and sat down in the same spot she had been in this morning when the commotion started. She felt like a part of some sort of bad dream that she couldn’t wake up from. She knew there would be some sort of consequences connected to this situation, and didn’t even want to think about what might happen.

Her servant Rhea came into the kitchen. “Rhea, did you have the Legate’s toga washed?” Livia asked.

“Yes, it’s almost finished and there isn’t a spot on it. Thank goodness for Nerva - even at her age she can still clean almost anything,” Rhea replied.

Livia looked at her dear servant and friend. She could see the fear and dread in her eyes also. She knew she must be strong for her and not let her own concern take over her emotions. “What would we do without her?” she replied smiling. “That woman’s skill is amazing.”

She wanted to distract her friend and give her something to do. "Rhea, please have all the lamps filled this afternoon. We will keep them lit throughout the night. The soldiers said they will take shifts sitting with him, and I doubt if the physician will sleep either," she said as calmly as possible.

"When you're finished, please come help prepare the evening meal," she continued.

"No one has eaten much today, and the men will be famished by nightfall."

Livia began to think about what to serve their guests and began to pray for wisdom as she planned. She would need every bit of it if she was going to help soften whatever consequences were coming to her family.

Chapter Six

Livia lay down on her bed; her head aching from the stress of the day. She had excused herself shortly after dinner and retired early. She knew sleep would not come while the sun was still up, but hoped the headache would ease if she got in a recumbent position. She placed a cold cloth on her forehead and stared at the ceiling, trying to think of something other than the guests in her home, but her mind would not let her. Instead, it just kept replaying the events of the day. She closed her eyes, hoping a different image would appear than that of the soldier holding Lucius Marius in his arms.

The entire day had a surreal quality about it. If she had not been wide awake, she would swear that this was a bad dream. Looking back, she could only think of a few days in her entire life that had been as difficult as this one. The sad part was that the day wasn't even over. If she thought the day had taken an eternity to pass, the night promised to last even longer. She knew she would not truly rest until she knew if their guest was going to live or die.

Her room was just across the hall from his and so she heard every movement that was being made. She heard the physician rise every now and again to listen to his patient's breathing and then talk quietly to the soldiers in the room. She had trained herself to listen for Stephanas's movements during the night, but as good as her hearing was, she could not make out the whispered words the doctor was saying. She had not disrobed in case she was needed during the night. She was so tired that she couldn't even pray, but she knew the Lord heard even her innermost thoughts, and tonight this especially brought her comfort.

She had lain there for a few hours and her eyelids began to get heavy. She was just beginning to fall asleep when she heard a long slow moan. It was followed by the words, "My head, oh-h-h-h my head!" She got up quickly and opened her door. She continued to hear the moaning as she crossed the hall and looked into the room where Lucius Marius lay.

He was holding his head with his hands, and was trying to focus his eyes in the dimly lit room. He recognized his guard, but did not recognize the doctor. "Where am I?" he asked as he attempted to sit up. "Who are you?" he asked as he looked at the doctor.

"Slowly, sir," the doctor said as he helped him into a sitting position. "You've been unconscious all day."

"And where exactly am I?" Lucius asked as he looked around the dimly lit room.

"You are in the home of one Junius Arvum," the older guard replied. His sheep were in the road as you went around the corner in your chariot. Your horses reared and you were thrown out of the chariot."

Just then Lucius noticed Livia standing at the door. He kept staring at her trying to make his eyes focus and his mind clear. Finally, he said, "Diana, what are you doing here in this strange place?"

"Sir, my name is Livia," she replied. Lucius refused to take his eyes off of her. Uncomfortable with his attention, she lowered her gaze and her cheeks reddened. She turned towards the doctor, "Is there anything I can bring your patient now that he is awake?"

"He may have just a little water with a small amount of wine in it," the doctor replied.

She turned and ran towards the kitchen. It was such a relief to have him awake; perhaps he wouldn't die after all.

She knew they were not free from danger yet, but this was a beginning. If he was speaking, surely his brain was not injured too badly. His mind seemed clear even if he didn't remember the incident.

She ran down the hall, and in her haste, almost missed her father-in-law sitting quietly in the atrium. He looked like he was praying. Her steps slowed and she turned to approach him.

He opened his eyes and raised his head. "Any changes in the patient yet?" he asked.

"He's awake, Father," she replied.

His sagging shoulders straightened and relief washed over his face. "Thank God," he said fervently. "How is he?"

"He's in pain, but he is talking and trying to make sense of where he is and what happened to him. The doctor said I should bring him some water mixed with wine," Livia explained.

As she returned with the pitcher of water mixed with wine, she quietly made her way into the bedroom. No one seemed to notice her as the doctor was making another examination of the patient. This time Lucius was making sounds as the doctor poked and prodded his body. Livia set the tray down and left as quietly as she had entered.

She returned to her room and lay down on her bed again. She closed her eyes and let her body relax. She could feel the weight of the day's events leave her mind. Lucius Marius would probably not die and that was all that mattered to her right now. She refused to let herself think about what might happen tomorrow. They had made it through today without another death in the house. Whatever came tomorrow, she would face. She was just grateful this horrible day had come to an end. She tried to pray a prayer of thanksgiving, but fell asleep in the middle of it.

It was still dark when Livia arose the next morning. She changed her clothes and put on a fresh tunic and stola as her clothes were rumpled from sleeping in them. She washed quickly, combed her hair, and put it up in a simple knot. She was a matron and no longer wore her hair down in the presence of other men.

As she approached the kitchen, she could see the first rays of sun coming through the window. Rhea was already in the kitchen and had put the bread in the oven to bake. They would need a few extra loaves today with the added company. She started slicing the fruit and the cheese so that they would be ready when the first person arrived for breakfast.

Junius was the first to arrive in the kitchen. He looked like he had not slept at all. Her heart went out to him when she saw his haggard face. "Let me bring you your breakfast - the bread is still warm from the oven," she offered.

"Thank you," he replied. He turned and went into the dining room.

She walked into the room and found him pensive in thought. "What now, Father?" she asked.

"We shall see what the doctor says, and what we need to do to help this man get better. He will be our guest as long as necessary and after that, well…we must make some kind of reparation for the accident. It was our sheep that were in the road, and who knows what will be required of us," he replied quietly.

She set a plate of fruit and cheese before him and also set a glass of fresh cold water at his place. She saw the worry in his eyes and started to tear up. He saw her eyes and took her hand. "We must pray, Daughter. Pray like you never have before, for we are now at the mercy of this man," he whispered.

Her hand began to shake when he let it go. She grabbed it with her other one to make it stop. She also knew they would be at the mercy of this man. He had the power and the authority to require whatever he wanted in recompense for the accident. What if he found out they were Christians? Although Christianity was tolerated at the moment, anyone could bring a charge against them, and there was not much they could do to defend themselves. There were still plenty of officials in the government who would welcome an opportunity to make life difficult for them.

They heard a noise in the hall as the younger soldier came around the corner into the dining room. "Do you have the Legate's tunic?" he asked. "He wants to dress and try to walk into the dining room for breakfast."

Livia brought the freshly laundered tunic and gave it to him. He examined it skeptically, but could find no fault in it. He turned to go back to the bedroom. "We shall be back in a few minutes," he said as he retreated down the hall.

Livia watched as he turned to go back to the bedroom. "Now it begins," she thought to herself. "Lord," she prayed silently, "give us wisdom to know what to do and help us find favor with this man. Help him to be merciful to us."

A little while later she heard Hector talking to Lucius Marius. "Slowly… slowly. There's no need to rush… your body has been through a great deal." He guided Lucius to the table and helped him sit down. He turned to Livia and said, "Bring him something light to eat. I don't know how his stomach will take to food."

Chapter Seven

Lucius Marius looked around the dining room. He had insisted the physician bring him to where he heard the people talking. He wanted to see whose house he was in and what the people were like. As he surveyed the room, he could see it was clean and it felt cool. There was a window open and a slight breeze was blowing in from the east. He turned to look at each person in the room.

He glanced first at Junius. He saw a man in his early fifties. He had the build of a man accustomed to physical labor. There was no fat on his body, and he seemed surprisingly fit for his age. He looked at Rhea, a woman in her mid-thirties. She was a little portly, but seemed robust and well able to work. And then his gaze turned to Livia, and his eyes stopped moving. He remembered seeing her last evening, but thought he had been dreaming. She was the spitting image of his deceased wife, Diana, when she had been in her late teens. She had reddish-brown hair, light olive skin and striking green eyes. There was a classic beauty about her face and it still had the innocence of youth. She was lovely to look at and yet there was an indescribable sorrow about her. He could see the curves of her body underneath her stola, and even in his weakened state, he felt aroused. He forced himself to take his eyes off her and turned to Junius. “Sir, I am Lucius Marius. May I know whose house I am in?”

Junius stood and introduced himself. “Junius Arvum, your Honor. I am sorry for the accident that happened yesterday; we are at your disposal to help in any way that we can. This is my daughter-in-law, Livia, and her servant,

Rhea. You have met, Hector, our physician. He is the finest in the area."

Lucius greeted each one with a nod. He then sat and Rhea brought him a plate of fruit, cheese and bread, and set a glass of water before him. He began to eat a few bites of the bread and cheese. He took a small sip of water to wash down the bread. "I'm afraid I am not at my best. My head still hurts a great deal and I am having a hard time keeping my balance. The physician assures me that this will get better in a few days, but says that I must stay here until I am fit to travel. He thinks I will be ready by week's end. I will need your hospitality for a few more days." He finished eating a small amount of the food that Rhea had put before him. Everyone remained silent as he ate. In a few moments he said, "I think I am ready to return to bed; all I can think of is going back to sleep."

Hector looked at him and said, "That is the very best thing you can do for right now. Your body needs time to heal from the fall." The physician placed his body under Lucius's arm and helped him rise from the chair. They returned the way they had come. As they walked into the bedroom, he turned him and gently eased him back into bed. "Sleep, your Honor; it will only make you better."

When Lucius awoke next, it was late in the afternoon. His head did not hurt quite as much as it had this morning, but he was beginning to feel the impact of the fall in other parts of his body. His back hurt and his right arm and leg felt stiff and swollen. As he started to sit up, the room began to spin and he had to stop moving.

The physician rushed to his side. "Let me help you, sir," he said. He eased him into a sitting position and then turned his legs toward the floor. Lucius sat there until he felt the dizziness leave. He wanted to stand and so Hector placed his body under Lucius' arm and helped raise him into a standing position.

"I'm ravenous," Lucius said, and then remembered he had not eaten anything since breakfast. He could smell something cooking in the house and it began to make his mouth water. "Walk next to me," he said, "I want to see if I can walk on my own." Lucius walked carefully out of the room and down the hall. They stopped in the dining room.

The older soldier, Gaius, who had been following his master's every step, turned and said, "I will have someone bring you something to eat."

"Remember, we are guests in their house, do not order them. Ask," Lucius said.

Soon Livia brought a steaming bowl of chicken stew with some fresh bread and placed it before him. He looked at her and let his gaze linger on her face. He then looked at the stew. "It smells delicious! I'm so hungry I can eat the whole bowl," he said with a warm smile.

Livia smiled back, but Lucius noticed she still had those same sad eyes. "I will be back with some wine and a pitcher of water," she offered politely.

When she was gone, Gaius asked, "Do we need to notify anyone in Ravenna of our delay?"

I don't think so," Lucius said, "they were not expecting us yesterday; they only knew we would be coming sometime this month. I don't want to send word unless I am here longer than I expect to be. The doctor said I should be ready to travel at the end of the week so a few days more or less won't make a difference to anyone at the house. I like to arrive unexpectedly to see if all is in order."

Gaius smiled grimly. He had seen the Legate angry and he knew if they arrived and things were amiss, heads would roll, not literally perhaps, but people would be out of jobs and servants whipped if things were not as they should be. He knew Lucius Marius to be a man of contradictions. He could be generous and kind or scathing and cruel, depending on his mood and the circumstances. He was still waiting to see what would be the outcome of this incident. Surely those responsible for this accident must know to tread very carefully if they were to emerge from this incident unscathed.

Lucius finished his dinner and turned to the doctor, “Physician, you’re excused for a while. I’m going to live,” he said wryly. He then turned to Gaius and said, “Help me walk around this house. I want to get my bearings and see where I am.”

As they walked the opposite way from which they came, he noticed the rooms were decorated quite simply. The furniture was in good condition, but it was nothing extravagant. The home was quiet and clean, thank the gods. With the pain in his head, he did not need children running around making noise or listening to servants bicker.

He went into the atrium where the servant Rhea was working quietly. She was humming a tune as she worked. Lucius thought it odd to see such contentment in a servant, but attributed it to the woman’s age. She turned as they walked past, still with a contented look on her face. “It would be nice if my servants were that contented,” he thought. “I wouldn’t have to worry about them stealing or lying to me.”

They stopped and Lucius sat on the divan. He needed a rest; he could feel the fatigue from just walking as far as he had. It wasn’t the tiredness like he felt last night after the potion the doctor had given him. That had sent him into blackness when he closed his eyes, and his dreams were disjointed and strange. He didn’t want any more of that medicine. And from here on out, he wanted a clear head. The pain wasn't that bad that it needed to be mitigated with the bitter herbal mixture.

They sat for a while and Lucius looked out the window. "This is really a beautiful part of Italia," he said. "I always enjoy coming back to my hometown on the coast." He saw the vineyard and the fields with the other crops. He could see a few servants moving about with their tools. "There is something to be said for an agrarian existence," he said, "as long as you don't actually have to live in the country and do the work." He was a city dweller through and through; the bigger the city, the better. He enjoyed the intellectual and artistic pleasures associated with living in a metropolis. He only came back to Ravenna when it was unbearably hot in other parts of the country.

Gaius stood and looked out the window for a few minutes. He heard the Legate breathing evenly and turned back to see him fast asleep. Should he keep him there and bring a blanket or take him back to his room? He decided he would bring a light blanket; his master would resent being carried back to his room like a child. He brought a blanket and covered Lucius with it. Gaius returned to the window and watched the shadows gradually lengthen as the sun moved over the hills behind them.

A few hours later Lucius awoke with a start. There had been something nagging at his mind ever since he woke from his fall last night. He knew he needed to do something important, but for the past day, he couldn't remember what it was. "Blast that potion the doctor gave me," he thought angrily. His head was finally clearing and he was no longer half groggy. He looked around the room and got his bearings. There was a lamp lit in the hall and its light was filtering into the room. He knew he had fallen out of the chariot and hurt himself. He knew he was in a farmhouse and that a doctor was taking care of him, and now his head cleared enough for him to remember why he and his guards had been racing down the coast road headed for Ravenna.

He had been in Mediolanum over a week ago, concluding business for the Senate. He had been getting ready to leave the stifling heat of the city for a few weeks on the Adriatic coast at his ancestral home in Ravenna. If possible, he tried to spend time there in the summer and a few days here and there, depending on his travels. He loved Ravenna and longed for it whenever he was in Rome or any other city where the heat was stifling and the air putrid. Ravenna was known to have one of the healthiest climates in Italia; for centuries gladiators had trained there because of it.

He was within days of leaving for Ravenna when an informant of his came to see him. She was supposed to keep an ear out for anything of interest that might help him politically. She moved in the highest circles in the city and heard secrets that many would pay handsomely for. She had an enormous appetite for the finer things in life, and she wasn't above selling what she had to acquire them. She came to him early one morning and told him what one of Constantine's generals had told her the night before. He drank more wine than he should have and she began to charm the information out of him. Constantine was indeed resting his army there this summer, but would move next month on Verona. After he had dealt with Verona, it was on to Rome.

Lucius had known that this might happen, but was unaware of the actual timing of the campaign. Lucius rewarded her richly for such an important piece of information and then accelerated his plans for leaving the city. He thought about which way he should go; should he go straight to Rome with the information or should he use this to his advantage while he was in the north of Italia? Not wanting to miss a chance to enrich himself, he decided to share the information with the officials in Verona and then those in his ancestral home in Ravenna. It would only take a few extra days and then he would turn south to Rome.

He sat up suddenly and the dizziness returned. He held his head steady to keep the room from spinning. He wanted to leave tomorrow but knew he was in no condition to travel. He looked at Gaius who was dozing silently in the chair opposite the divan. He cursed the gods for his inability to travel and be on his way; it was almost as if they were trying to stop him on his quest. Thinking further along those lines, he began to feel guilty about his mission.

He knew the senators in Rome hated the Emperor Maxentius. Maxentius held little regard for them in return. He was brutal and had taken many a home or wife from those of the upper class in order to gift them to a praetorian or some other official he wanted to reward. The most notorious story about him involved a woman named Sophronia. She was the virtuous wife of the Prefect of Rome and Maxentius had given her to one of his subjects as a reward. When the time came, she stabbed herself to death rather than be taken by him. That incident served only to make the senators hate him all the more.

He began to ask himself why he was helping the man everyone hated. Even his own father, who was known to tolerate the excesses of the emperors, especially loathed Maxentius. Lucius's head cleared and the answer was crystal clear.

He knew beyond a shadow of a doubt why he wanted to reach Rome and warn Maxentius. The way things were, he had little chance of getting in the Emperor's good graces and elevating himself in the political hierarchy. The Emperor disrespected the Senate and had little to do with them. With this information Lucius had a chance of gaining favor and position for himself and his family. Who wouldn't make this choice if they were in his position? With that rationalization, Lucius calmed his guilty conscience and thought about what to do next.

The room was silent and dark, and Lucius did not feel he could walk back to the bedroom by himself. He lay back down slowly - his head full of the possibilities of gain that were set before him. All he wanted was to get well so that he could be on his way. He would rest and hopefully feel better tomorrow. If only he could make the cursed dizziness leave! He started to get angry about this delay. Someone should pay for this accident, and he began to think about what he would like in the way of compensation. A picture of Livia came into his mind and he began to smile. Perhaps this delay would work out for his personal benefit after all!

Chapter Eight

It had been a week since the accident with Lucius Marius. Livia was aware of each hour as it passed; time seemed to have slowed these past few days. She waited with expectancy to see what would happen to them when this important man's visit came to an end.

The Legate was almost ready to travel. He walked further and further each day in order to gain his strength back. He told the doctor that his head hurt less each day and the dizziness was better. The doctor continued to come daily, and today had announced that Lucius Marius could leave tomorrow if he wanted.

Livia had asked Junius this morning what they would do to make reparations for the accident. He told her he didn't know. He had spoken with Lucius a few times about it and Lucius had not given him an answer. Junius told her that until they made reparations of some sort, they wouldn't be able to put this incident behind them.

The last few days Lucius had asked her to walk with him and show him their property. He was respectful to her as he asked her about her late husband, Stephanas. She had shared with him how they had met, and how the marriage had taken place. She told him that they had truly loved each other and that it had not been a marriage of convenience. He was also very inquisitive about the way they ran the household and the estate. He had never seen servants who were so willing to work and had such a positive attitude towards their masters.

She told him that about ten years ago Junius had given all of the household and farm slaves their freedom. Only those who wanted to stay and work could; the others could leave and go wherever they wanted to. A few had left, but the ones who stayed did so because they chose to. They had quarters to live in and food to eat each day. When the crops were sold, each individual got a small amount of the profits for the year. No one was rich, not even them, but they all worked together and there was no vying for position with Junius in the fields or with herself in the home.

She conveniently left out the fact that they were Christians, and that was the real reason for the harmony in the home. They worshipped together on the first day of the week and kindness and honesty were the mainstay of the household. Of course, they had not had their gathering this past Sunday because Lucius and the soldiers were there. She didn't think he was suspicious of their beliefs, as his main focus had been on getting better and stronger each day. Livia's reverie was interrupted as she heard the sound of someone walking towards the kitchen. She turned and saw Lucius Marius coming through the door.

"Livia, come walk with me today," he said.

It was not really a command, but Livia knew she must not refuse his request. She put down what she was working on and wiped her hands on a towel. They stepped out onto the veranda and began to walk towards the fields. She was unprepared for what came next.

He took her hand and said, "How would you like to come and live in my home in Ravenna? You could help manage my household."

She was dumbfounded and could only stare at the fields ahead as she took in the enormity of the request. She remained silent and did not answer.

"My home in Ravenna does not run as smoothly as this one. The servants quarrel and bicker and my steward is constantly having to discipline them. I know they steal from me, even though he seldom catches them. I think that you could bring some order and peace to my home. My steward is getting older and is exasperated with the female servants."

She continued staring ahead and her stomach began to churn. She had only lived two places in her entire life and they had both been warm homes where she was surrounded by people who loved her and believed as she did. "But what of Junius and the home here?" she asked quietly.

"He has been asking me for days what he could do to repay me. I have thought and thought and there is nothing here materially that I want or need. My real need is to have peace and quiet when I return home and to know my home is in capable hands." He waited for a few moments and then said, "With your approval, I will speak to him this morning about it."

She knew she was walking on dangerous ground and the welfare of her household probably depended on her answer. She quietly prayed and thought for a few more moments as they walked. She felt she was resigned to this fate because of the accident. She thought about it and then spoke. "I will come if Junius approves," she said quietly and without conviction.

"Good, then it's all but settled," he smiled and said. "I will pay you well to be the matron of my home and you will want for nothing. Who knows, you may not even want for affection if things work out right." He took her hand and squeezed it as they continued to walk.

Her stomach began to tighten and she felt nauseous. She would be little more than a hired servant who would be expected to give her master her body on occasion. The thought of spending a night in his bed sickened her. It went against everything she believed in, and she started to feel numb.

She looked around at the sky and the trees. Nothing had changed in the past few moments, and yet everything looked different. The beauty of the day had dulled, and the tasks she had planned to do seemed suddenly unimportant. She felt bereft and even more alone than she had when Stephanas had died. At that moment a thought occurred to her, "May I take my servant Rhea with me?" she asked hesitantly.

"Of course," Lucius said, "I want you to feel comfortable in your new home. I'm leaving tomorrow and Junius can bring you into Ravenna the following day. My servants will prepare rooms for you both and I will let them know to expect a new mistress. I know they will be pleasantly surprised when they get to know you, as I have been."

They continued walking and then turned back towards the house. Livia began to feel a numbness sweep over her. She said nothing as they walked and would not let herself cry as she thought about leaving her home.

"Look, there is Junius," Lucius said, "I will go and speak with him now. The matter will be settled within the hour."

He left and she continued walking and entered the house. She could not look at Rhea as she worked; instead she went straight to her bedroom. She lay on her bed and wept silently. She felt she had lost everything when Stephanas died, but now she was really going to lose everything; her home, the people she loved, everything…everything except Rhea. She must tell her; her life was about to change, also. She got up, washed her face and went to find her dear servant and friend.

Rhea took one look at her and saw she had been crying. "What is it, Mistress Livia?" she asked.

Livia took her hand and led her into a room where no one could hear what she was about to say. "We're leaving, Rhea, and I don't know when we are coming back," she said with resignation.

"What are you saying?" Rhea asked with a shocked look on her face.

"I'm the payment the Legate wants for the accident," Livia replied.

"But Master Junius would never let you go," Rhea said resolutely.

"I already said I would go," Livia explained, "and he is settling it now with Junius. I really have no choice, and father Junius knows it."

Rhea looked as stunned as Livia had been at the turn of events. "Surely there is something else we can do," she whispered.

"No, there is nothing else he wants. He told Junius as much." she countered. "We will be leaving day after tomorrow. Don't say a word to anyone until father announces it to the household, and don't look angry or afraid around the Legate. I am going of my own free will and you will have to also, if you will go with me. I won't force you to go."

"You don't even have to ask me, you know that wherever you go, I will go with you," Rhea said. "I've been watching over you since you were a child, and I'm not going to stop now, especially under these circumstances."

Livia felt grateful for the determination in Rhea's voice. "Dear, dear Rhea," Livia said as she embraced her. "What would I do without you? And now, dear one, return to your work. Tonight and tomorrow we will pack for our new home. Let us pray, we will need to pray much to get through the next few days."

Chapter Nine

Junius froze in his tracks as he saw Lucius coming towards him. Lucius had a grin on his face and he was waving at him. Junius had seen him and Livia walking a few moments before, and he wondered what they could be talking about. He had felt uncomfortable the last few days as Lucius had asked her to walk with him around the property. It bothered him to see this older man take such a personal interest in her.

"Ah, Junius," Lucius said, "I think we have resolved the problem of restitution that you keep insisting on. I have asked Livia if she would come and work for me and help make my house in Ravenna run as smoothly as yours."

Junius was taken aback at the statement. He didn't want to believe his ears. He had thought that perhaps some form of monetary restitution would be agreed upon as the Legate seemed to have no interest in any of the crops or animals. He had not let himself imagine that the man would want Livia. The thought was repugnant to him. "What did she say?" he said evenly. He could feel his anger rising and he forced it down.

"She agreed and said if it met with your approval, that she would come. She asked if she could bring her servant, Rhea, with her," he said smiling. "What a fortunate thing this accident has turned out to be. I have a house where the servants are always bickering with each other and they seem to have a surly attitude much of the time. I know your daughter-in-law can work wonders with them. I will pay her well and she will want for nothing while she is in my employ."

"And how long do you have in mind to keep her?" Junius asked, trying to keep his face from showing how he really felt.

"As long as she will stay. I would think she could do wonders in a few months, but I would like her to stay at least a year with me," Lucius replied.

Junius remained quiet and thoughtful. He was not in a position to argue with this man who had been injured by his sheep. Lucius Marius was from the most prominent family in the region, and he had the power to demand recompense any way he wanted it. He wasn't demanding it; he was asking, but Junius knew he was not in a position to refuse him. The thought galled him, but there was nothing he could do about it. A few moments later he said dully, "If she has agreed, then she has my permission to go."

"Good, then it is settled. Please bring her and her servant in day after tomorrow. I will only be in Ravenna for a few more days and I would like to introduce her to the household before I leave. They will need to know that I have chosen her and they must obey her and do her bidding," Lucius replied.

Junius watched him turn and walk away. His anger and frustration were growing by the moment, and he needed to be alone to think. What could he do to stop this? How could he have been so stupid these last few days when he had seen Lucius walking with Livia? Why hadn't he seen that the man had a plan and a purpose towards her? His body suddenly felt old and his shoulders slumped. He felt defeated as he walked towards the barn. He had promised his son that he would take care of his wife when he was gone, and now this. She was like a daughter to him and she was being ripped away from him and his household. As he entered the barn, he saw Gaius brushing the Legate's horses.

"Good morning, Junius," Gaius said. "We will be leaving here tomorrow morning, and I wanted to make sure the horses were ready to go. I hadn't noticed any problems after the accident, but I wanted to check their legs and hooves one last time before we left."

Junius kept his anger in check again. "I'm glad your horses are in good shape. If you have need of one of ours, we will be glad to give you whatever you need," he said earnestly.

"Yes, I'm sure you would," Gaius replied. "You are most fortunate that the Legate has recovered so well. Who knows what would have happened to you and your estate if he had been severely injured. As it is, he seems impressed with your daughter-in-law and he can't seem to take his eyes off of her. You are indeed blessed by the gods that he wants to take her into his house."

Junius was surprised that Gaius knew about Lucius's plan before he did. He felt hurt, anger, and totally impotent to do anything about the developing situation. He was losing his daughter-in-law to a man who would probably expect more from her than she was willing to give. It would not end well – that much he knew.

"You have nothing to say to that?" Gaius asked inquisitively.

"I lost my son a few months ago and now I am losing my daughter-in-law," Junius replied guardedly. "I am at a loss to respond at the moment."

"Of course," Gaius said. "Any father would be proud to have his daughter-in-law in the Legate's home, but you are surprised by the turn of events. I am surprised myself that he would be interested in someone beneath his class, but you must admit, she is a rare jewel. She is pretty to look at, and she is not loud and vulgar like many of the women who pursue the Legate. She seems industrious and totally without guile. Your servants respect her and she seems to be able to manage the household well at such a young age."

"Yes, you are right. I am surprised by the turn of events," Junius said as he turned to go. His anger was turning into rage and he needed to get out of there fast before he said something he would regret.

Gaius stared at him as he retreated out the door. He wondered why the man was not happier at his good fortune. He continued brushing the horse. Some people just didn't know how fortunate they were!

Chapter Ten

Livia arose early the next morning. She had slept little during the night as a multitude of thoughts and emotions vied for her attention. Her concern for her future was trumped only by her sorrow at leaving her home. She hated leaving it because it was where she and Stephanas had spent their life together. She noticed that her face was red and swollen when she looked into the small mirror he had gotten her as a gift. She took a cloth and dipped it into cold water, hoping to undue the effect of the crying she had done as morning approached. That done, she proceeded to dress and head to the kitchen to help with breakfast for the household and the departing guests.

As usual, Rhea was in the kitchen ahead of her. She looked like she hadn't slept so well either. Both of them worked without saying much; as of yet the rest of the household did not know about the turn of events. A short time later the servants came into the kitchen for breakfast. Livia looked at them lovingly and wondered when she would see them again.

As soon as Lucius and his soldiers came into the dining room and were seated, Livia and Rhea went out to serve them. Lucius looked especially well this morning, and was smiling every time his eyes landed on Livia. He looked at her as if he was pleased with his new acquisition. Sometimes his eyes lingered too long on Livia as she went around the table to pour water for the men. Her face reddened at his attention and she had to force herself to finish the job before she left the dining room.

A short time later the men left for Ravenna, but not before Lucius called her aside and told her how much he was looking forward to having her in his home. It took all of Livia's reserve to remain calm and thank him for this opportunity to be of service to him and his household. Lucius arched his eyebrows at this comment; his surprise showing on his face. Livia didn't know what he expected of her, but she was not going to show him her true feelings. She especially did not want to show him any sign of fear.

Livia saw the guests to the door and then walked through the house quickly. Once in the kitchen she walked to Rhea's side and spoke softly in her ear. "I will be back in a while, but there is something I need to do before we go." She walked out the back door and through the fields.

She looked at the fields, trying to memorize a picture of them in her mind. She didn't know when she would be back and she didn't want to forget this place she had come to love. At last she came to the end of the property where the crypt was. She sat down on one of the benches outside of it and just stared at the door. Nothing could make her go in there, but she wanted to be as near to Stephanas as she could without actually going inside.

She wept again as she thought of the years she had had with him and how they had ended. She wanted to tell him she would always love him, no matter what came to pass. It was important for him to know that, and she believed that somehow he was looking down from heaven and he could see her where she was. Unexpectedly, she felt a sense of peace and knew that somehow the Lord had conveyed her thoughts to him. She stayed there for a long time and then began to tell herself she must go back to the house. No matter what she said to herself, though, she couldn't make herself leave her husband not knowing when she would be back. There was a rustle in the grass behind her and she turned to see Junius walking towards her.

"I thought I might find you here, Daughter," he said.

She stood and turned towards him. "I couldn't leave without saying goodbye one last time."

"I come here many times to talk to Prisca; it makes me feel closer to her," he said. He looked at her face and took her into his arms. Livia wept and the tears fell on his shoulder. "I haven't been able to tell you how angry I am at the turn of events. I never wanted this to happen to you. If only Stephanas were alive…well, if he were alive this would not be happening to you." He released her and looked into her face.

She could see the agony in his eyes, and wanted to ease it. "True, but who knows what price Lucius Marius would be exacting from you instead," she replied.

"It couldn't be higher than the one I'm paying now," he said dejectedly.

Livia searched for something to say to him that would help him feel better but she could think of nothing.

Junius spoke again, "I came to get you for the noon meal. Rhea and I have shared with the servants what is taking place. It's a good thing we waited until after the Legate left to tell them. Several of the men are quite angry and old Claudius wanted to fight him himself.

Livia smiled for the first time since yesterday. The thought of Claudius wanting to fight Lucius was comical. Sometimes Claudius could barely keep his balance when he walked, let alone try to fight someone. It did make her feel good that the people in the household cared so much for her. She loved them and she was grateful they loved her in return. "Dear, dear Claudius," she said chuckling.

"We missed our Sunday gathering with the guests here, and we would like to spend some time in prayer for you and Rhea after the meal," he said.

"What would I do without all of you and the Lord?" she asked.

"What would we all do? If it wasn't for the Lord, I am afraid of what I might have done to that man yesterday when he told me he wanted you to go with him." Junius said. "I could have strangled him on the spot."

"Who knows what that would have meant for all of us," she replied.

"I know," he said. "I haven't had a chance to tell you that he is only going to stay in Ravenna a few nights after you come and then he is leaving."

Relief flooded her mind at the news. Surely this was a sign that God was working in the midst of this difficult situation. The thought of him not being there made the situation almost bearable. "That's more than I dared hope," she said, a spark of joy blossoming in her soul. Perhaps her time there wouldn't be so bad after all.

They turned and walked back to the house. Junius's shoulders were still bent with the strain of worry, but Livia felt a renewed confidence in the Lord and His provision for her. They walked into the kitchen and then into the dining room. Everyone was seated at the big table and the food was set before them. Junius sat at one end of the table and Livia sat at the other.

Junius prayed a prayer of thanksgiving for the food and the dishes were passed. Everyone ate in silence, each contemplating the situation. Livia could not stand the morose atmosphere and she wanted to break the silence. "Father Junius has just given me some good news," she began. They all looked up from their meals not knowing what to expect. She looked in each face and then smiled, "Lucius Marius will only be in Ravenna a few nights and then he will leave on another journey." A few let out an audible sigh of relief. "Rhea and I will covet your prayers each and every day. It will only be with your prayers and the help of the Lord that we will make it through whatever we will encounter in his home."

They all started to talk at once. "Of course, you will have our prayers, Mistress Livia," Nerva said. "If only I could go in your place," she added.

Livia looked around at them, tears filling her eyes. She and Rhea were not alone in this. These dear faithful people would be holding them up in prayer daily and she knew they would be close in spirit. "Thank you," was all she could say without breaking down. She looked at Rhea's face and she could see that she was also trying to hold her emotions in.

The meal continued until they had all eaten. Rhea went and got a loaf of unleavened bread and put it at Junius's place. Livia poured a goblet full of wine and placed it beside the bread. They bowed their heads and Junius began to pray. He then thanked the Lord for His sacrifice and he broke the bread and passed it around the table. He took a drink of the wine and passed the goblet also. Junius then began to pray for Livia and Rhea. Each person at the table said a short prayer for them also. The finality of this last time in prayer together began to overtake Livia's thoughts. She could not concentrate on what was being said and sorrow began to well up in her soul. Her eyes filled with tears again. When would she be able to gather with other believers again? Only the Lord knew the answer to that question.

Chapter Eleven

Livia listened to the gentle clip-clop of the horses' hooves as they traveled the road to Ravenna. She was lost in thought and did not speak much to Junius. She had resigned herself to her fate and had prayed for the strength to make the move without grieving outright today - so far, so good. She saw the Porta Aurea[11] and knew their time together was short. Despite the warmth of the day, she felt a coldness inside as they neared the entrance to the city.

They came through the gate into the city and continued on. They traveled through the forum and she marveled at the statue of Hercules. She saw the statue of General Marius and she looked at it intently, trying to find a resemblance in the face to that of Lucius. She saw the Temple of Apollo and the Amphitheater. They were almost to the place where they would separate, and now, there would be one last tearing away. This morning she felt she was being torn from her home, her beloved family, the servants she loved and the beautiful countryside.

They crossed the bridge and Junius stopped the wagon by the main canal, the Flumen Padena. There were boats waiting to take passengers wherever they wanted to go in the city. She had brought a small amount of money to pay the fare. Lucius Marius had told her to have the steward pay the man when they got to his home, but she wanted to pay it herself. It might be her last act as a truly free woman.

Junius came around, took her hand, and helped her out of the wagon. She could barely look into his eyes for fear of crying. He held her for a moment and she let out a

---

[11] The Golden Gate was the only entrance by land to the city of Ravenna. In centuries past, it had been covered with gold.

muffled sob. "I know I've said this to you many times in the last few days, but there must be another way to pay this debt," he said.

"If there was another way, the Lord would have shown it to us," Livia replied. "I trust Him even if I don't understand any of this," she continued.

He then helped Rhea out of the wagon and helped load the two small trunks onto the boat. He then helped Livia and Rhea in. "You both are in my prayers. We will keep in touch some way, I promise," he said.

"Where to?" the porter asked.

"Do you know where the home of Lucius Marius is?" Junius asked.

"We all know where his house is. We haul many supplies and important people to his residence when he is in Ravenna," the porter answered. He looked them over carefully as if trying to determine what business they had with the Marius home. He started to say something but stopped. He then began to steer the boat away from the dock.

Livia gave Junius a half-hearted wave as the boat departed. She watched him until they were out of sight of the dock. She then began to look around as they traveled the canals. She had never been in this part of the city before. When they came to town to shop, they had always gone to the Caesarea district, a suburb outside of the walls. This was an entirely new world to her. She knew the city had quite a history and that its port had been vital to Rome in times past. She never would have imagined that she would be living in this place, however.

The porter pulled up to the Marius home. It was indeed large and very impressive. Suddenly, she felt small and awkward. She looked at her clothes and those Rhea had on.

They were clean, for sure, but there was nothing fine about them. Their garments were made out of a simple cotton fabric with very little decoration on any of them.

The porter tied up the boat at the dock and helped the two women out. He took their trunks and set them on the dock. Livia paid him and thanked him for his service.

"I will go to the door and see if there is someone who can help take these in," he grunted. He knocked at the door and an older man answered. "I have two women and their belongings on the dock," he said.

"Ah yes, we have been expecting them," the older man replied. "Let me get some money to pay you," he continued.

"No need," the porter said, "the younger one of the two paid me herself."

The older man looked at her inquisitively. "Now here is a different kind of woman," he muttered quietly. He walked with the porter to the dock. "Welcome, my name is Mago; Master Lucius told us to expect you sometime today. Let me take you to your rooms where you can get settled in. I will have the servants bring your trunks in. Master Lucius will be glad you are here," he said.

The last statement made Livia's stomach turn. From now on Lucius would be her master, also. The thought made her feel nauseous and she felt her stomach flip-flop as they followed him down a long hall and up a set of stairs. He led them to two rooms, one next to another. Livia breathed a sigh of relief; she and Rhea would be close together.

"These are your rooms. I hope they will meet with your approval," Mago said.

Livia looked around her room. There was a bed and cabinet for her clothes; there was a dressing table with a mirror attached to it and a decorated pitcher of water on one end, and there were towels folded next to the pitcher. The furniture was finer than any she had lived with. Next, they walked into Rhea's room. It was about half the size of hers but it was also nice. There was a bed and a cabinet for her clothes, and she also had a small dressing table, water and towels.

"This is more than adequate," she said smiling.

"Good, then I will leave you two to get settled in. I will let Master Lucius know your rooms met with your approval," he said.

When Mago left, they walked around the rooms together. They looked out the windows and could see other fine homes across the canal. They could also see the skyline of the city. "We're not in the countryside anymore," Livia said wistfully as a small tear ran down the side of her cheek. She wiped it away quickly before Rhea could see it.

"No. No, we're not," Rhea agreed as she continued looking out the window.

Just then they heard a knock at the door. Rhea went to answer it. Two younger men were each carrying one of the trunks. "Where do you want me to put this one?" the darker one asked.

"In here," Rhea answered, "the other one goes in the mistress's room next door."

Livia returned to her room to put her clothes and her few belongings away. She placed the mirror Stephanas had given her on the dressing table. She poured some water in the basin and began to wash the dust from the journey off her face. Just then there was another knock at the door.

It was Mago this time. He held a tray with cheese, bread, fruit and two glasses of wine on it. "Would you like something to eat? Dinner won't be for another few hours and you both are probably tired and hungry from your journey," Mago said.

Livia was surprised at the consideration she was being shown. She didn't know what she had expected, but it wasn't to be treated with kindness. She viewed herself as another hired servant - nothing more. "That is so considerate of you," she said. "Thank you so much. Rhea and I appreciate your kindness very much."

Mago smiled. "I will send someone for you in a few hours. You will have dinner with Master Lucius and your servant Rhea will eat with the rest of the servants in the kitchen. I know this is all new to you, but I want you to feel at home here," he said warmly.

"Perhaps, I shall find a friend here after all," she thought to herself. She knocked on Rhea's door, went in, and shared the tray of food with her. They ate with relish as they had not eaten anything since before they left early this morning. Livia could feel herself getting sleepy and so she excused herself and returned to her room. She was just going to lay on the bed for a few moments but closed her eyes and fell fast asleep. The next sound she heard was a quiet knock on the door. She looked around the room and remembered where she was. She got up quickly and went to the door. She heard the gentle knock again.

"Mistress Livia, I am here to take you to dinner," a feminine voice said quietly.

Livia opened the door and saw a girl no more than fifteen, waiting for her. "One moment, please," she said, "I must have fallen deeply asleep." She turned and knocked on Rhea's door. Rhea was also resting on her bed. "We will need a few moments to freshen up," she said to the girl. Livia changed her clothes quickly and fixed her hair. She didn't want to offend Lucius Marius on the first day she was here. The girl waited quietly as they readied themselves.

"I am Iris, and was born in this household. My mother served the Marius family her entire life," the young girl said proudly.

They began to walk through another long hall that took them away from the bedrooms and into the living area of the house. They passed a library several times the size of their small library at home. At last they came to a room with an ornate table in it. Lucius was reclining at the table waiting for her. There were several trays of food already on the table. He pointed to the couch across from himself where he wanted her to recline.

Rhea followed Iris as she continued walking towards the kitchen. She looked back at the scene and gave Livia a worried look. Livia raised her eyes towards heaven; their secret signal to pray. Rhea nodded and walked on towards the sounds coming from the kitchen.

Chapter Twelve

Marcus was unloading barrels of wine from the provinces. He was almost finished when he turned and saw his father walking towards him. The look on his father's face told him everything and nothing. Obviously, there was more bad news, but he couldn't imagine what it was. He put down the barrel and walked towards his father. "What's wrong, Father, is it Claudius? Has something happened to him?"

His father shook his head and sighed. "Is there somewhere we can go to talk privately?" he asked.

"Let me put these last few barrels away and then I will see if there is someone who can watch the warehouse for a while," Marcus answered. He quickly unloaded the barrels and shut the rear door of the warehouse. As he walked to the front, he saw Otus, a trusted servant of his uncle's.

"Could you please watch things for a while? I need to go with my father. I'll be back shortly," Marcus said.

"Of course," Otus responded.

Marcus and Junius walked out the front door. "Father, what has happened that we can't discuss it at the warehouse?" Marcus asked.

"It's Livia," Junius replied, "she is no longer with us."

Marcus stopped abruptly. "What are you saying, Father? Don't tell me she's dead!"

"She's not dead, son, but I don't know when I will get to see her again," Junius replied.

"You're talking in riddles now. Please tell me what has happened," Marcus said exasperatedly.

"A little over a week ago some of our sheep broke through a fence and were in the middle of the road. Lucius

Marius and two of his soldiers were coming around the corner at full speed. Lucius was in the front with his chariot, when he ran into the sheep. He was thrown from the chariot and knocked unconscious.

They brought him into the villa and put him in Stephanas's room. We sent for Hector, our physician, and Hector stayed beside his bed until he awoke that night. It seems Lucius has a head injury of some sort. He had some dizziness and a bad headache, and it took him several days until he was well enough to travel. I don't know how long the effects of this accident will last.

While he was with us, he took an interest in Livia. He liked the way she looked and he appreciated the peace that was in our household. He does not know we are believers and so attributed the peace to Livia's expertise with the servants. When he was better, he spent several hours talking with her. It made me uncomfortable, but there was nothing I could do about it.

Every day I would ask him what I could do to make reparations for the accident. He didn't seem to be interested in any of the crops or animals or even an offer of money. The day before he left, he and Livia were walking in the fields. On his way back to the villa he came to tell me he had come up with a solution to the question of reparations."

"Don't tell me," Marcus interrupted, "he wanted Livia."

"I'm afraid so," Junius continued, "he wants her to come and manage his household. She knew the position we were in, and so she consented to his request. He wanted her to come within a few days. I just came from dropping her off at the dock - a porter took her to the Marius house. Fortunately, he let Rhea go with her, so she is not all alone there."

Marcus was stunned by what he had just heard. He walked along in silence for a few moments as he tried to take the news in. He knew of the man's reputation; he had delivered wine to the Marius home many times, and had heard remarks about some of the events that had been held there.

"She'll be like a sheep in the den of a lion," Marcus said defensively.

"My sentiments exactly," Junius replied. "I told your brother I would look after her, and now I feel I have betrayed my promise to him. The man doesn't have a wife, and I don't think Livia is safe around him. I don't know how she will react should he ask for more from her than she wants to give. She could soon be in great peril."

In Marcus's mind, he began to think about that unpleasant scenario. His emotions began to catch up with his thoughts and he felt a strong sense of protectiveness towards her. He could see why she had consented to go. She wanted to spare his father and the rest of the household any repercussions from the accident.

"I tried to talk her out of it," Junius continued, "but she didn't feel there was any other answer. She said she was what he wanted and so she must go. What if she feels she must give him her body in order to protect us?" He paused for a few moments and then said dejectedly, "It's almost too much for me to think about."

The thought of Livia lying in Lucius Marius's bed against her will made Marcus angrier and angrier. He knew the man would not have the decency to marry her. She was below his social class, and he would view her as an expendable item when he tired of her. No matter what her fine qualities were, she would always be little more than a servant to him.

Marcus kept walking in silence. He wanted to rescue her from all this, but for the moment he knew he must calm down, think clearly and plan carefully. He turned to Junius and said, “Father, we do business with the Marius’s. We keep them supplied with wine, so we deliver there often. His steward comes to the warehouse when they are having a special dinner and he orders whatever he wants. I will go when we make the next delivery and I will see if I can talk to her and find out how she is doing.”

“The Lord be praised! At least we have a way to check on her and to keep in touch with her,” Junius exclaimed.

“We must tread carefully,” Marcus cautioned, “Does he know you have a son working in this part of the city?”

“No, he never asked me about my family,” Junius replied.

“Father, we must get her out of there. We must come up with a plan that allows her to escape. He is a powerful man and his tentacles reach far, so it will not be easy, but surely there must be a way,” Marcus said thoughtfully.

“I wish I could believe that,” Junius said. He sounded more hopeful than he had been in the last few days. “I have thought of nothing else, but nothing has come to my mind. He knows where we live, so we cannot bring her home, and she is not safe around here. He has too many eyes and ears here in Ravenna.”

“Last week when we delivered wine, his steward said he would only be here a month this summer and then he would be gone until spring. Perhaps she is safe for the time being,” Marcus suggested hopefully.

“Perhaps…perhaps, we do have some time to think and plan,” Junius remarked thoughtfully. “Lucius told me himself that he would only be in Ravenna a few days.

Marcus's eyes brightened and they turned to walk back to the warehouse. Both men were silent and determined as they strode back. Marcus noticed there was a lightness in Junius's step that had not been there before their conversation.

As he walked, Marcus began thinking about the two things he had not wanted to have anything to do with in the past few years - Livia and the Lord. The thought struck him that he would never be able to help Livia without assistance from the Lord.

They returned to the warehouse and Marcus told his father goodbye. He helped close the warehouse and asked Otus to tell the family that he would not be coming for dinner. Marcus began walking on the road that would take him down to the beach along the Adriatic. He wanted to be alone so he could think about his relationship with the Lord. To say it was strained would be an understatement; he felt it was practically nonexistent. Marcus knew he had pushed the Lord away for years, but it had not always been that way. He remembered the times as a child when he attended services with his parents. His parents had taught him and Stephanas much about the Lord and he used to enjoy listening to the stories about Jesus and the apostles.

He wondered if he had ever really accepted their religion? Did he believe that Jesus Christ was God's son and that He had come to earth to die for the sins of the world? Did he believe that He was crucified for those sins and that God had raised Him from the dead on the third day? Did he believe that He ascended into heaven and He was ruling and reigning there at this moment? Marcus thought about those things for a long time and finally decided he did believe those things to be true, but that was not really the crux of the issue with him.

Marcus knew that if he asked Jesus to come and live in his heart that he was going to have to make him the Lord of his life. He was going to have to give up the right to his own life and become a servant of the Lord. He was going to have to quit going his own way and seek the will of the Heavenly Father. He knew it beyond a shadow of a doubt because he had seen it modeled in his father, mother and brother. As his father would say, he was going to have to "take up his cross daily, deny himself and follow the Lord."

Those were not light words to Marcus. He walked and walked as he wrestled with his emotions and his will. Was he really ready to give up the life he was leading and follow the Lord? Marcus was not sure - he was going to have to think long and hard before he made that kind of a commitment.

Chapter Thirteen

Livia was quiet as she reclined at the table. A servant served food from each tray to her. Lucius sat across from her smiling smugly. "So, you are finally here at last," he said. "I have been waiting for you all day. Did you find your new arrangements satisfactory?"

"They're more than acceptable. You live in a very beautiful home, Master Lucius," she replied. She had never addressed him that way before, but since she was in his employ, she would show him the respect he deserved.

"Please call me Lucius. I hope that we can become friends, perhaps even more than friends while you are here," he said. "I hope you become fond of your new home and that you desire to stay here for a long time."

Livia was not taken aback by this disclosure; she had been wondering what he really wanted from her when he requested she come live in his home. "Sir, I am still a grieving widow, and for the moment I cannot think beyond the one I have lost."

"Of course, of course," Lucius said. "I expect nothing more for now. I know it will take time to get over your grief. For now, you can learn to run my home with the same skill you showed at your father-in-law's. I liked the way things ran smoothly at Junius's home, and how the servants respected you. I would like you to bring that same peace and order here. Mago has always managed the servants, but as he has gotten older, he has lost all patience with them. He yells and screams and has become harsh with them for little or no reason and they have become sullen. No one is happy or contented here - they just serve because they are forced to."

Livia couldn't share that all of the servants at her home were believers and that they had a common goal - that of pleasing the Lord. They worked together, and because of their beliefs, those in charge did not feel they were any better than those who served them. "It will be a difficult task to bring a new way of doing things here, but I will try to do my best," she said.

"I'm sure you can work wonders with them," he replied. "Tomorrow, I will have Mago take you to the market. You will need some new clothes if you are to serve as the matron of this house. One of our servant girls is very good with hair, and she can fix yours in a more appropriate style for your new station. Perhaps you would even like to try some of the cosmetics that some of the Roman matrons wear."

Livia's face reddened and she inadvertently put her hand up to her face and hair. She felt even more out of place than she had when she arrived.

He saw her hand move to her hair and face. "There is nothing wrong with the way you look - it's fine for living in the country," he said reassuringly, "but you will be living in the city now and you will be expected to dress and look differently if you are going to bring credit to this house. The servants must know that you are truly above them if you are going to get the respect you will need from them."

Livia had just taken a bite of food and could hardly swallow it. She looked at her hands - she had never paid much attention to them before, but she noticed that they were red and rough from her work in the kitchen. Her eyes started to water, and she wondered what she had gotten herself into.

Lucius noticed her response and he reached across the table to touch her hand. "Don't be frightened. You will do just fine here." He turned and made a motion for the servant behind him to bring him something. "I've been waiting to give you this," he said as he motioned for the servant to bring a small tray to her with a necklace of pearls on it.

Livia gasped. "I can't accept these from you. I just got here and you don't even know if I'll be able to do any of the things you want me to."

Lucius smiled, "They're just a gift," he said. "I had Mago pick them up yesterday for you. I just want to say thank you for accepting my offer and for coming."

Livia felt herself sinking inside. She felt like he was attempting to purchase her. It would be so easy to betray everything she had ever lived for, if she wasn't careful. She took a few deep breaths. Lucius got up and walked around the table. He took the necklace off the tray and put it around her neck. His hand lingered on her neck for a moment too long. He walked back around the table and looked at her approvingly. "It looks lovely on you Livia; just like it was made for that slender neck of yours."

Livia placed her fingers on the necklace. She had seen slaves wearing collars in the market place. The collars were ugly and she always felt compassion for those who wore them. Now she had her own slave collar; the necklace felt heavy as she rolled the pearls between her fingers. "Thank you," was all she could say.

"I'm leaving for Rome in a few days. I had meant to spend several weeks here, but something has come up. I will spend the winter there working with the Senate. I should be back early in the spring. I hope to find a transformation in my household when I return. I'm trusting you to work your magic here, Livia," he told her.

Livia looked at him. "A reprieve," she thought. "God has granted me a reprieve from him." She continued picking at her food. It was no use - she couldn't eat. "May I be excused to return to my room?" she asked hesitantly. "There has been so much excitement today that I'm feeling quite exhausted from everything," she explained.

"Of course," he said. "You may not see much of me tomorrow as I prepare for my journey. I hope to take dinner with you every evening before I go. Tomorrow Mago will take you and your servant to the shops. He will help you decide what you will need while you are here."

Livia rose and walked slowly back to her room. She became disconsolate as she approached her bedroom door. She was thinking of Lucius's hand on her neck when a picture of Stephanas came into her mind. She knew she had not betrayed him but felt guilty nonetheless.

Rhea had heard footsteps approaching. She cracked her door to see if it was Livia. She saw the forlorn look on her face and hugged her. It was then that she saw the necklace. "He gave you a pearl necklace?" she asked. "Whatever for?"

Livia looked at her sadly and nodded. "It's my slave collar. Mago purchased it yesterday for me in the market." Tears welled up in her eyes and a few rolled down her cheeks. "It makes me feel like he is trying to purchase my affections."

Rhea just held her as she sobbed silently. Rhea turned her into her room and helped her disrobe. She helped her into bed and placed the covers over her. "Thank you," was all Livia said, but she knew the look in her eyes spoke volumes to Rhea.

Chapter Fourteen

Livia awoke early the next morning. She had slept fitfully the night before. All she could think about was what Lucius Marius would eventually want from her. She tossed and turned as she thought about how she would answer him and what his response might be. The Lord had given her a reprieve from him for several months while he was in Rome. She appreciated the distance that would be between them, but she knew that eventually there was coming a day of reckoning with the man.

She got up and began to pour water into a bowl so that she might wash her face and arms. There was a quiet knock on the door and she opened it to find Iris standing there. She was carrying a light blue tunic and stola made of an exquisite material and a small pair of hand tooled leather sandals.

"The Master asked that I bring you these to wear today, and asked that I would take care of your hair every morning," she offered. She lay the garments on the bed.

Livia looked at the stola. She had worn a beautiful stola on her wedding day, but that material did not match this for quality. She looked at the sandals; a decoration was neatly tooled in them. She noticed there were a few small stones set in them and they looked like they were about her size. She cast a glance over to her own sandals. They looked rough and worn in comparison to them. "I can't wear these today - I'm going to the market with Mago," Livia protested.

"You're going to be the matron of this house, my lady, and you must start dressing like it," Iris explained. She slipped the tunic and stola over Livia's head and had her sit in the chair by the dressing table. She then began plaiting her hair and artfully placing each braid on top of her head.

Livia was uncomfortable with someone fixing her hair. She had always done it herself and had finished it within a few minutes each morning. It seemed like Iris was working on it for an interminable amount of time.

Rhea knocked on the door softly and let herself in. She let out a gasp of surprise. "You look like one of the wealthy ladies in the marketplace," Rhea exclaimed. She watched Iris as she continued working on the back of Livia's hair. Rhea reached for the mirror and held it in back of Livia's head so that she could see what her hair looked like. Livia let out her own gasp of surprise.

"I hope you're pleasantly surprised, my lady," Iris said as she finished the last few curls.

"Thank you, Iris," Livia said, "Rhea and I will be down shortly to eat something."

"Good," Iris replied, "I know that Mago wants to get an early start. He hates dealing with the large crowds that come to shop later in the day." Iris left as quietly as she came in.

"Amazing," Rhea said. "The dress and those sandals must have cost Lucius a small fortune."

"To us, yes," Livia said, "but to him it may not be much at all. Who knows what will be bought in the shops today."

Livia placed her feet in the delicate sandals and walked over to where Rhea was standing. "Let's pray before we start this day."

She took Rhea's hand, "Lord, please help us today. We are walking into the unknown and we don't know what we'll be facing. Please give us your wisdom and discernment as we go through this day. Amen."

They gave each other a final look and headed out the door. Livia felt uncomfortable in such fine clothes, but she was determined to learn her role and her place in this home. They walked down the hall past the dining room and into the kitchen. As they walked in every eye fell on Livia, but no one said a word.

Mago looked at her approvingly. Livia had been transformed into a woman who looked like she had been raised in patrician circles. "I see Iris has done her work well," he remarked.

Livia looked around at each one seated at the table and then began to introduce herself. "My name is Livia, and I look forward to meeting each one of you. This is Rhea, I know that you met her last night at dinner. She has been my servant since I was a child."

Her kindness disarmed each one of them. They did not know what to expect when they had been informed that their master was bringing a new woman in to be the matron of the house. They knew she would be in charge of them, but they had no idea how they would fare under her hand.

Mago turned to each one and introduced them to her. "This is Argia," he began, "she is in charge of the kitchen." He pointed to a large heavy-set woman in her middle years. Her hair was pulled back in a bun and her face was red. "These are her two daughters, Cora and Clio - they help her in the preparation of all of the food." The two young women looked up and smiled. Livia noticed that they were younger, slimmer versions of their mother.

He pointed to Iris. "You've met Iris," he said. She will help you with your preparations and she attends all female guests who come to this home. She is skilled in the art of cosmetics and beauty. She will help take care of your clothing and will launder your clothes for you."

He then turned to his right and extended his arm to two women sitting on the other side of the table. This is Leda and Jocasta; they are in charge of cleaning the master's house."

Livia looked from one woman to the other; both appeared to be in their middle years and each had a few strands of gray in their dark hair. She smiled at each one; they in turn nodded timidly.

Mago looked across the table and introduced Phylla, and Maia. "These two women do the rest of the laundry for the household."

Livia noticed that they both looked about her age, but all had a muscular build. "No wonder," she thought, "the muscles they must have from doing such heavy work."

They were not afraid to greet her, though. "Welcome, Mistress Livia. We look forward to serving you," they said in unison as if they had practiced it. Mago gave them a scowl as they giggled after they made their statement. Paying no attention to him, Livia rewarded them with a big smile.

Mago then turned and introduced the two men who had carried their trunks in, "This is Trachis and this is Erebus. They help with the heavy work."

Both men looked to be in their twenties. They were well built and attractive in their own right. Livia thought they could easily cause competition between the younger women in the household. She smiled at each one of them in turn.

The servants resumed eating the morning meal, but the kitchen was much more subdued than when Livia and Rhea arrived. Mago then guided her into a small adjoining dining room. Her breakfast was brought to her and she ate alone. When she was finished, a servant sent for Mago.

He had asked Trachis to port them to the shops this morning. She and Rhea got their cloaks and went to the dock. The four of them entered the boat and they set off on their prescribed errand.

It was the second time in two days that Livia and Rhea had been in a boat. They took in the beauty of the city as the small boat glided silently on the water. They had always shopped in the suburb of Caesarea, closer to the port at Classis - it was much cheaper than buying anything in the smaller shops in the city. She noticed that the weather was cooler here than it was in the country. The wind blew in from the Adriatic and kept the temperature moderate in the city. It was especially cool this morning and Livia was glad that she and Rhea had worn their cloaks.

They stopped in front of a small shop that sold yardage. As they docked and began walking towards the shop, a few people on the walkway stared at her. They seemed curious about who the woman was with Mago. Livia thought he must be well known in the city as the steward of the Marius home.

"Welcome, Mago," the merchant said as they entered his establishment. "I haven't seen you here in a long time. To what do I owe the pleasure of this visit?"

"We are shopping for the Lady Livia today. Could you please show us what you have that would be appropriate for everyday wear and also for more important functions in our home?" Mago said.

The shopkeeper eyed Livia and began pulling bolts of cloth down from his shelves.

"Let's start with this for every day. I have just gotten in this shipment from Egypt. The Egyptians make the best cotton and their dying techniques are second to none." He held each one up to show Livia and to see how the color looked against her skin.

"These are good," Mago said. "Do you approve Mistress Livia?"

"How could I not? The material is of excellent quality," she said.

"And now show us what you have for a more important occasion," Mago requested with an air of authority.

The shopkeeper went to an area behind him and brought out bolts of diaphanous material. "This is stunning if it is placed over a tunic that sets it off," he said.

Livia's jaw dropped as she fingered the lovely material. Again, the shopkeeper took the bolts and held them up near her face to find the colors that were complimentary for her.

"Would your wife be available to take the Lady's measurements?" Mago queried.

"Of course, please come this way," he replied.

Mago nodded at Livia as she and Rhea were led up the stairs to the shopkeeper's home. His wife looked up from her work. She was cutting some material out on a large table.

"Would you please take the Lady's measurements?" the shopkeeper asked. He turned and left the women to themselves.

She took her measuring string and started getting the needed measurements. She looked into Livia's eyes occasionally, but Livia gave nothing away. When she was finished, Livia said, "Thank you." She and Rhea then descended the stairs to the main part of the shop.

"Everything is taken care of," Mago said. "The finished garments will be delivered as soon as they are ready." The shopkeeper was smiling and thanking Mago. He waved to the two women as they exited the shop.

"Did that meet with your approval?" Mago asked.

"I don't know what to say," Livia began to protest.

Mago hushed her. “There’s nothing to say. We are following the master’s wishes. We have one more stop to make and then we will return home.”

They began walking down the street and soon stopped in front of a small shop that sold sandals. This was not the run of the mill shop; there were sandals on display that had jewels and beading on them. Mago looked around and smiled. “Ah, this is what I had in mind.”

They walked into the shop and at the sound of their entrance the shopkeeper came out from behind a curtain. As he did, Livia saw men making sandals in the back part of the shop. Mago looked at a few of the designs and had the man measure Livia’s foot. The shopkeeper brought out several styles for Livia to choose from. Livia picked out a few but couldn’t bring herself to choose any more than two; it all seemed so extravagant to her.

Mago could see her hesitation and picked out a few more and then he and the shopkeeper discussed the price. Livia raised her eyebrows as she heard them discuss the cost. She was stunned as Mago paid the sum.

Livia was silent as they began to walk back to the boat. The whole experience had taken a few hours and Livia felt the fatigue of the last few days settle on her. She felt uncomfortable in her new role. To say she felt totally out of place would have been an understatement. After a while she said, “Do you shop here often?”

“I used to come to these shops with Mistress Diana when she was alive,” Mago replied.

“What happened to her?” Livia asked.

“She died in childbirth several years ago. She was a beautiful, kind woman, and we miss her greatly. I thought Master Lucius would go mad from the grief when she and the baby died. He’s never been the same since. He gets little pleasure from the ladies that try to curry his favor and take her place," he explained.

Livia felt a wave of compassion for the man. "I understand a little of what he must have gone through. I lost my husband a few months ago," she offered.

"I know," Mago said. "Master Lucius explained your situation to me before you came. You know. Livia, it's uncanny the way you resemble Mistress Diana."

Livia was dumbfounded by the revelation. She remembered when Lucius had first seen her and called her Diana. Could this be the real explanation for the situation she found herself in?

"Oh," was all Livia said, but she was thinking "Oh dear!" as she entered the boat.

Chapter Fifteen

The next few days were a flurry of activity for all in the household. The master was preparing to leave for the winter and all the necessary preparations were being made. Each day Livia and Rhea would spend the day with a different group of servants to learn how they performed their activities and what the household schedule was.

Lucius took every meal, except for dinner, on the third floor. His private living quarters were there and he spent much of the time reading his correspondence and making preparations for his trip. When it came time for dinner, he asked Livia to share the meal with him in the large dining room on the second floor.

She was becoming accustomed to this routine and always let him lead in the conversation. She was careful about her answers as he quizzed her on her day's activities and what she was learning about the servants. They had been on their best behavior for her and she had glowing reports to relate to him. He seemed satisfied with the interest she took in her new duties and the seriousness with which she applied herself in learning them.

The last evening before he left, he seemed more concerned for her welfare than he usually was and wanted to make sure she was adjusting to her new environment. "Tell me, Livia, are you missing your home in the country terribly?" he asked with genuine concern in his voice.

"With all the things I have to learn, I haven't had time to think of it much," she answered honestly.

"Good," he replied. "I was hoping you would find this a pleasant home to live in. As you know, I will be leaving in the morning. When I return, I hope to find you fully settled in and a regular part of the household. Mago will release authority for the women servants to you bit by bit as you feel ready to take over the responsibility for them. He has told me that you have been working alongside them every day in order to learn their responsibilities."

"Yes, I have," she said. "I feel the best way to establish a relationship of trust with them is to show them that I am willing to work alongside them and learn their duties."

"I never had any intention of you doing hard labor with the servants when I brought you here," he countered, sounding sterner than he wanted.

"If I learn how they are supposed to do things, then I will be able to correct them if I see something out of order. If I don't learn the right way to do the work, I will not be able to make any corrections or suggestions should I see something amiss," she replied.

"Interesting," he said with a smile. "You're not afraid of hard work. Most women I know would run from it."

"I worked with the servants in the kitchen at Junius's home and I will probably work in the kitchen here when I learn all of the responsibilities. There is a lot to do to feed all of the people in this household and I want to be a part of helping with that." she said.

He shook his head. "No wonder your servants were so contented. You worked right alongside of them. Don't you feel that you are above them?" he asked.

"No, not at all," she answered. "The important thing is that the household runs smoothly and that the master of the home is pleased with the work that is done."

His patrician sensibilities were taken aback. He looked at her closely. She was so unlike the women he met socially. They wanted to be waited on hand and foot and they gloated about their station in life. They appreciated the fact that they didn't have to lift a finger to work and that others were there to serve them. Here was a woman who looked like she actually enjoyed serving others.

"You could actually make me believe that you like the work you are doing." he said.

"I do like the work; of course, not all of it. I won't spend long with those doing the laundry, but I do like to see a house kept clean and I do like planning meals and deciding what is going to be served," she explained. "I also like getting to know each person and learning a little bit about each of them."

"And what have you learned?" he asked inquisitively.

"Not much for now," she replied. "They don't know me yet and won't tell me much of anything." Treading carefully, she said, "May I ask you one question before you leave?"

"Go ahead," he said, surprise showing on his face.

"Are you still feeling the ill effects of your fall?" she asked, the concern evident in her voice.

"I still have the constant headache, but it is not as severe as it was in the beginning. My double vision is almost gone and I am seeing things normally now. I do have occasional episodes of dizziness each day, but they only last a short while," he told her.

"Again, I am so sorry for that unfortunate accident." she said.

He could see that she was truly concerned about him and it pleased him. "I don't look at it as so unfortunate. It has delayed my trip a few days, but I met you, and now you have come to share my home with me. I would like to take you to Rome with me, but it isn't the right time. You will do better learning the things you need to here," he replied.

Livia kept her face impassive. Inside she was beginning to wonder where this accidental encounter would eventually lead. She didn't want to be someone's mistress or concubine, no matter how important they were or where they would take her.

"Would you like to go to Rome with me?" he asked.

"I am having trouble learning all I need to here in Ravenna," she answered discreetly.

"A wise reply," he said. "You already look and act different than you did in your country home, but it will take time to adjust to living in a different social class than the one you have been raised in. You will do better here this winter, but know this, I will miss seeing you. You have already brought a sense of peace to me and my home."

She had no response to his personal remarks about her. She remained silent for a time, relieved that he had chosen not to take her with him. She had no desire to leave Ravenna and go even further from the family she knew.

He got up, went behind her and kissed her on the cheek. He let his lips linger on her face and she could feel his warm breath. "I wanted to say my personal good-bye to you this evening. I will look forward to seeing you in the spring, dear one." With that he said goodnight, turned and walked out of the room.

Livia remained reclining at the table. She could still feel his warm lips on her cheek and placed her hand where he had touched her. She recoiled at the thought that he was beginning to be more intimate with her and noticed that the servant in the corner of the room was watching her carefully. She did her best to not give away her true feelings.

The servant came to help her rise. "You are fortunate that our master is so fond of you. It's too bad he can't stay longer this visit."

"Too bad, indeed," Livia replied, a little too quickly.

She turned to go to her room, grateful that he had only offered her a kiss this evening. Stephanas's face again came to her mind and she felt guilty that Lucius had kissed her, even if it was just on the cheek. She lowered her head as she walked and wrapped her arms around herself. She didn't want to think of how she would feel if he had offered more of himself to her. For tonight she would be thankful Lucius would be leaving in the morning.

Chapter Sixteen

Lucius Marius paced around his family's home in Rome like a caged animal. He was becoming rabid about seeing the Emperor Maxentius. He and his bodyguards had made haste for Rome the moment they had left his house in Ravenna. They had made the trip in a little over a week and Lucius was still feeling the strain of it.

He was also feeling the effects of his fall and had pushed himself on the trip in order to arrive in Rome as speedily as possible. The information he held was too valuable to stop unnecessarily. He had arrived in Rome three days ago and had requested a private audience with the Emperor, stating that he had vital information that was necessary for the security of the empire. He was becoming increasingly agitated the longer he awaited the Emperor's reply.

A few hours later a messenger came with the Emperor's reply; he would be seen this afternoon. Lucius made his final preparations and had the driver bring his chariot to the front door. He sat down on the seat as the driver began the trip to the palace. The air was hot and humid and Lucius began to sweat as they made their way through the streets. Normally he would be annoyed at the weather and the stench it brought, but today he was buoyed by the opportunity to advance himself into the Emperor's good graces.

They arrived at the palace and Lucius was escorted into a room by a Praetorian guard. He was asked to wait and the Praetorian stationed himself outside the door. The moments dragged on…fifteen minutes, half an hour, and then an hour. "Didn't anybody know how important he was and that he might have something important to say?" he thought to himself. Lucius kept talking to himself to keep his temper under control. He did not want to appear peevish when he finally got to see Maxentius.

The door opened ahead of him and he was led into another rather large room. He stood hoping that the Emperor would appear momentarily. When he didn't appear after a quarter of an hour, Lucius began walking around the room looking at the beautiful frescoes. He was gazing on one showing Bacchus at play in a forest with a few wood nymphs when a door opened at the far end of the room. Maxentius entered with one of his Imperial Guards.

"Ah, Lucius Marius, what brings you here today?" he said.

Lucius bowed and began, "Your Excellency, I would not have disturbed you unless I had information of the utmost importance."

"In these times, I am appreciative of any information from loyal subjects like yourself," the Emperor replied.

"While I was in Mediolanum my sources told me that Constantine was making plans for a campaign that would take him to the very gates of Rome," Lucius said.

"This is not new information," Maxentius said.

"Yes, Excellency, but a source has told me the timing of the campaign and the route he plans to take," Lucius replied.

"What do your sources tell you?" Maxentius asked, looking a little bored.

Lucius was caught off guard by Maxentius's reaction. The man acted like he was hardly interested. "He will leave for Verona in September to fight General Pompeianus and the forces stationed there," Lucius said, "then it's on to Rome."

"Yes, that is what my sources have told me also," Maxentius replied.

The air left Lucius's lungs and he had to deliberately take his next breath. He began to feel defeated. He thought this news would be greeted with alarm and that he would be rewarded for coming so speedily to Rome. He wanted the man to know he had come in all possible haste to tell him this news. "I heard this and immediately came to tell you myself," was all he could say.

"Yes, I'm sure you did, and your loyalty will be rewarded," Maxentius said graciously.

Lucius began to take heart and smiled. Perhaps there would be a reward for his effort after all. "Thank you, Excellency," he replied. "I knew you would want to start preparing immediately for the defense of the city."

"I am confident our forces can easily defeat his in battle," Maxentius said.

An alarm went off in Lucius Marius's head. "Did not this man know that the best defense was to stock the city full of supplies and close the gates of Rome?" he thought to himself. He must tread carefully. Who was he to advise the Emperor on how to defend the city? "Of course, they can," Lucius replied cautiously.

Maxentius looked at him, "What can I do to reward you for your loyalty?" he asked.

Lucius was still in shock that Maxentius was thinking of fighting the army of Constantine instead of starving him and his army out. Everyone knew that the surrounding countryside could only support an invading army for so long: sooner or later the invaders would have to leave. Closing the gates of Rome had worked before in the city's long history, and it could work again.

It appeared that Lucius was unwilling to ask for anything. Maxentius asked the question again, "What can I do for you to reward your effort on Rome's behalf?"

Maxentius did not realize that Lucius had been distracted and had not heard the question the first time. Lucius heard the question the second time and his head began working on the answer. He had hoped for a generous reward, but that wasn't going to happen; perhaps he could further his ambitions a little here. "Your honor, as you know, I am a Legate for the Senate. If you find the need for an Imperial Legate, I would be delighted to serve you in a greater capacity."

Maxentius looked at him for a long time. He hadn't expected a request to move the man up politically. He had hoped a material reward would be requested from him. He didn't want to refuse him outright because the man had made an effort to reach him and tell him of the information he had. "I will keep you in mind, Lucius, but you know that in your services for me you would have to travel a lot further than you do now and the danger increases the further you get from Rome," he replied.

"It would be an honor to serve you and Rome in any way I can," Lucius said.

He knew he was being put off and he started to seethe.

"Thank you, Lucius. You will be hearing from me soon," the Emperor lied and turned to leave.

Lucius watched him walk out of the room. He knew he had been dismissed and he then turned to leave. He had come with such hope this afternoon and he was leaving with little more than an empty promise of reward. His mouth felt dry and his shoulders sagged from the disappointment. A Praetorian guard met him upon leaving the room and escorted him until he was outside the palace.

Lucius's chariot and driver were waiting for him as he exited. "Home," was all he said. His mood grew darker and darker the further he got from the palace. He had come to Rome in the middle of August when the heat was at its worst. Now here he was, a month earlier than he normally came back, and he was sweltering while most of the senators were in the countryside enjoying relief from the heat. Well, he wouldn't stay. His father had a villa outside the city and he would leave for there as soon as he could.

He wanted to hurt someone and make them pay for this injustice. He had put out so much effort and was not being rewarded for it. They pulled up in front of his house where one of the servants was clearing up the remains from a broken clay pot. Lucius got down from the chariot and came over to him. The man could see he was angry and began to cower. Lucius did not even ask him what happened; he just slapped him as hard as he could and walked off. Having done that, Lucius felt immediately better.

Who else could he give a thrashing to? He walked through the front door looking for someone to take the rest of his wrath out on. He looked around and started to walk toward the library. There was a servant sweeping the floor and Lucius noticed the man had missed a small area of dust. He went over to him and slapped him hard. "Idiot," he said, "you've missed some dirt." He walked off without a single misgiving.

Lucius entered the library and slammed the door. He wanted to be alone and think.

He was angry that he had left Livia in Ravenna. He had so wanted to sample that delicious morsel and he gave it up to come here. For what? For this! For nothing! He sat in his chair and his head began to throb. He sat for what seemed like hours and didn't move. His anger began to dissipate and he again allowed himself to think about Maxentius and his plan to bring his army out to fight Constantine's army. What a fool the Emperor was if he thought that was the best way to defend the city. Surely nothing good would come from it. He would at least warn those he could so that his friends and family would be ready for whatever came.

His mind turned to another tack. Perhaps he could get word to some of the senators and maybe they could convince the Emperor to take another course of action. He would have to be very careful, though. If word got back to Maxentius and he was perceived as trying to criticize the Emperor's plan, he would lose what little favor he had with him. A servant came and announced dinner was ready. Lucius got up slowly from his chair. He was exhausted from the events of the afternoon and the emotional toll they had taken upon him. He finished his dinner and went to his room to lie down and rest. He consoled himself that he would leave for the countryside tomorrow. He knew the Imperial Legate position would never be offered to him.

His mind began working on a plan to survive the coming invasion, and then the thought struck him; of course, he didn't want to be an Imperial Legate. If the power structure changed, he would be perceived as being too close to the defeated Emperor. No, he would keep his distance from Maxentius and would gladly welcome Constantine into the gates of Rome when the time came. He was done with Maxentius and would sit back and watch his defeat. At that thought, Lucius smiled, closed his eyes and went into a sound, dreamless sleep.

Chapter Seventeen

It had been almost three weeks since Lucius had left for Rome and Livia's life began to fall into a regular pattern. She would rise a little before daylight and pray, afterward she would wash and dress for the day. Iris would come in and do her hair and then she and Rhea would go to the kitchen. Argia would be there baking the day's bread. Her daughters would be busy preparing the first meal for the household.

Mago would be the next one in the kitchen. She and he would go into the small dining room and have breakfast together. They would discuss the menu for the evening meal and any special duties that needed to be taken care of that day. She had a special request for him today. She wanted him to show her the first floor and the quarters where the servants lived. She told him that she wanted to make sure their living quarters were clean and in good repair. Mago looked like he was taken aback by the request, but consented grudgingly. They finished breakfast and went to the first floor.

As they were walking through each of the rooms, Livia noticed that the walls needed some plaster to repair the cracks and they needed a new coat of whitewash. In general, however, the rooms looked fairly tidy. It was obvious that the servants didn't own much.

"What would it take to get these walls repaired and whitewashed?" she asked Mago.

"Mistress Livia," Mago began, "I don't know why you care about the servants' quarters. They have been this way for years."

"That's just my point," she said. "I wouldn't want to live in a bleak and cheerless place and I'm sure they don't either."

When he could see that she had her mind set and would not be dissuaded, Mago said, "I don't think it would cost too much. The men could do the plastering and painting. The supplies aren't terribly expensive; I could report it to the master under necessary repairs."

"Good," she said smiling.

Just then someone knocked on the back door of the house. "It's probably one of the merchants making their deliveries," Mago explained. He turned and walked to the door.

Livia stayed where she was; she continued looking at the walls and the state of the rooms. She was deep in thought, wondering what else she could do to make them more comfortable for the servants.

Mago came back and said, "Mistress Livia, there is a man at the door who would like a word with you. He says he's a relative of yours."

Livia walked to the door and was shocked to see Marcus unloading barrels of wine. After a few seconds, she said, "Mago, this is Marcus, my brother-I…"

Mago interrupted her before she finished her sentence. "Your brother? I've known Marcus for many years. He has come often to this home to deliver wine."

Marcus looked at Livia and stared at her as if waiting for her to correct Mago's mistaken idea of who he was. Livia didn't say a word. Marcus took his cue from her and said nothing also. He stared at her and tried to take in this new picture of his sister-in-law. Her hair was plaited and she was wearing a beautiful stola. She had been transformed into a patrician lady since the last time he had seen her.

She spoke in order to break the uncomfortable silence. “Would you like to come in? I will go and ask Argia to prepare you something to eat and drink.”

“Yes, of...of course,” Marcus stuttered, his face growing red.

“Mistress, let me go and have something prepared for your guest,” Mago said. He turned and left.

When she was sure Mago was out of earshot, she turned to Marcus, “What are you doing here?” she asked.

“We deliver wine to this house routinely,” he replied. “I came this morning on the deliveries hoping to get a chance to see you and find out how you are doing.”

“So far it’s not as bad as I thought it would be. Everyone has been kind to me and I am learning my duties,” she offered.

“Livia, I can’t believe this has happened to you. My mind cannot fathom that so much could change in our family in such a short time,” he replied.

She smiled and shook her head sadly. “I know; I can hardly believe it myself. How is our father, Junius, doing?”

“The last time I saw him he was upset and worried about you,” Marcus told her.

“Yes, he was that way the last time I saw him also. Marcus, please, come and have something to eat and drink,” she said.

He walked behind her and looked around at the house. In the past he had only been on the first floor where he unloaded the full barrels of wine and took the empty ones back to the shop. Now he was on the second floor, being served by one of the women who worked in the kitchen.

Livia looked at Marcus and felt really homesick for the first time since she had come to the Marius home. His eyes caught hers and she tried to stop the tears welling up in them. She waited for Argia to leave the room.

"How often do you come here?" she asked.

"Every month, depending on what your steward orders in the shop," he answered. He hesitated for a moment, then said, "I can be in the area every few weeks and stop and check on you if you wish."

"Yes, I would like that," she said. She looked at him wistfully. He had worked away from home for so long that she hardly knew him. Stephanas had known him and loved him and now she was seeing him as if for the first time. He was dark skinned with dark hair and piercing brown eyes. She felt attracted to him and it surprised her. She turned away, hoping he would not sense her feelings. "Let me go and tell Rhea that you are here," she said, hoping to get away from the nearness of his presence. "She will be as happy to see you as I am."

"No. Wait, please." he whispered and caught her hand. "Don't go yet. Tell me how you are really doing."

She felt the warmth of his hand and her heart began beating faster. She stumbled on her words. "I…I'm fine. Master Lucius has gone to Rome for the winter, so I don't think I am in any real danger from him. When he comes back that may be a different story," she answered, acutely aware of his nearness.

He continued holding her hand. "That's what I am worried about," he told her.

Tears welled up in her eyes again. "I don't know what can be done. I don't want our family punished for such an unfortunate accident. I've thought this over a hundred times and I see no other answer," she said, resignation heavy in her voice.

"There must be an answer somewhere. Are you praying?" he asked quietly.

"Rhea and I are both praying, but so far nothing has come to our mind. In fact, the longer I am here, the more I seem destined to be part of this place," she continued.

"Don't even say that," he said adamantly. "I can't stand the thought of you being close to that man. We all know what he is like."

Livia was surprised by the intensity of his feelings. She felt a sense of protection like she felt when she was with his brother. She and Marcus had been casual acquaintances and she had not thought he cared that much for her. Now he was showing a level of concern towards her that she would not have imagined.

Just then Rhea came into the room. "Master Marcus, how are you?" she said.

He gently released Livia's hand. He looked disappointed by the intrusion. "I am fine, Rhea. I have come to see how you both are doing," he answered.

"As you can see, we are quite well taken care of," Rhea answered, motioning towards Livia wearing her new apparel.

Livia was embarrassed and changed the subject. "Marcus, we need to let you eat and drink while you are here."

Marcus began to eat a piece of bread and drink the small glass of wine that was set before him. He continued eating in silence until Rhea left the room.

"I will come every few weeks to visit you. You will be in my thoughts," he said quietly as he looked at her.

Livia was surprised and pleased that Marcus would be thinking of her.

"I must go," he said as he finished eating. "I must finish my deliveries and get back to the shop."

Livia was disappointed he had to leave so soon. He stood up and followed her back the way they had come.

Mago was still downstairs checking their stores. He looked at Marcus and said, "Come again, Marcus, I can see that Mistress Livia was happy to see you."

"Thank you, Mago, it was good seeing Livia and Rhea," he said. He turned and picked up an empty wine barrel, then headed for the door.

"Please come again," she said, as Marcus walked past her.

Marcus turned and saw the sadness in her eyes. "I will," he promised.

Mago also saw the sadness in Livia's eyes. "Come, let's go back to the servants' quarters and finish our discussion," he said as he closed the door.

Livia followed him slowly down the hall, her mind full of thoughts of Marcus. She felt alive again for the first time in months. She forced herself to concentrate on what Mago was saying but she barely heard him for the thoughts whirling around in her head. When Mago finished talking, she said, "Good, let's get this done soon before the heavy rains start for the winter. Everything will take longer to dry when the dampness really sets in."

She turned and headed upstairs to her room. She found herself smiling as she walked.

Marcus had made her want to hope. Even if there was no way out of this situation, she still wanted to hold hope in her heart for a while. She looked out the window to see if she could see his boat on the canal. He was nowhere to be seen, and she felt disappointed.

She looked in the mirror and straightened a curl. Her face looked flushed and she suddenly felt young again. She had felt so old these past few months. “Every few weeks, I will be able to see him every few weeks,” she said to herself excitedly.

Chapter Eighteen

Marcus left the Marius home in a state of bewilderment. He had been prepared to see Livia, but he wasn't prepared to see her looking the way she did. She looked beautiful and in control; she looked and acted as though she fit in the residence she was in. His sister-in-law's quietness now appeared to be a dignified reserve. She exhibited a sense of dignity as she walked around her new home.

He began to ask himself how he could have been so blind? This woman had both inner and outward beauty, and he had missed seeing it before today. So, this is what had drawn Stephanas to her? If he had given Livia a chance, he may have seen a lot more fine qualities in her. Marcus could not believe how attracted he was to her; and to think a few months earlier he had rebelled against the prospect of marrying her. Had he ever been mistaken!

He continued to row to the next residence, all the while thinking of what he could do to get Livia and Rhea out of that place. He must go see his father tomorrow and talk to him about it. He knew his uncle would give him a few days off and he couldn't wait to mount his horse and get on the road.

Early the next morning he was off and on his way to his father's home. He stopped again at the spring to water his horse and reflected on what he was feeling the last time he was there. Never in his life would he have believed his feelings would change for Livia in such a short time.

As he continued on his journey, he thought about what could be done to get Livia out of the Marius home. Where could they go that would be safe? How could they get away without being found by Lucius? How far would they have to go to be away from his reach?

Marcus entered the house and found his father working in the library. He greeted him and then said, "Father, I delivered wine to the Marius home yesterday. I saw Livia and Rhea and was able to speak with both of them."

"How did you find them? Are they well?" Junius asked.

"Surprisingly well," Marcus began. "Father, you wouldn't believe it. Livia looks like she's from a patrician family. She was beautifully dressed and her hair was all arranged.

She was talking to the steward like she had been there for years. Rhea also looks well."

"Did you see Lucius Marius?" Junius asked.

"He's already left for Rome. Livia said he's going to be gone for the winter. She feels that she is safe for now.

"Good," Junius replied looking relieved.

"Father, I am here to talk about what we can do to help them get away from him.

I've been thinking about it since I saw them. I have an idea, but it will take some planning and some money to get them far enough away from there."

"Go on," Junius said.

Marcus continued, "It's dangerous for everyone involved. Who knows what Lucius would do to you and the others if he came home and found her missing?"

"What do you have in mind?" Junius asked.

"Passage on a ship for the three of us. We could go to Carthage and disappear within the Christian community. There are thousands of believers in the city, and I know we could get help from someone once we got there," Marcus explained.

Junius was thoughtful for a while. “You’re right,” he said, “anything we do is dangerous once Lucius finds out that she is gone. I will gladly risk what I have for her, but I must talk to the servants here to find out if they are willing to risk their livelihood also. We may all have to pay a heavy price when and if the time comes.”

“That’s the problem,” Marcus said. “We can help Livia, but then everyone else is subject to Lucius’s wrath. Who knows what the man is capable of?”

“Today we will tell them that we are thinking of something to help Livia and Rhea.

They will be told it could cost them and they must think about it seriously. They are all free, and may want to go their own way when the time comes,” Junius said thoughtfully.

“There are other problems, Father. It will soon be winter, and we won’t be able to get on a ship until early in the spring. There’s the money, also. It will cost a lot to buy passage for the three of us, and then we must get them out of the house and away from there without anyone knowing we are leaving.” Marcus said.

“Yes, we must think, pray and plan carefully,” Junius replied. “First, we must give our servants the choice to go or to stay, for once we are committed to our plan, there will be no turning back.”

Junius was thoughtful for a few moments and then continued, “Marcus, I am pleased that you have been working on a way to help Livia. I know you were angry with me when I discussed leaving her half of the property.”

“I was angry, Father,” Marcus said. “I thought you were trying to make me marry her and I didn’t like it at all. Everything changed when you came in and told me what had happened to her. I began to feel protective towards her and then when I saw her yesterday, my feelings changed. I want to take her for my wife, Father. I know it sounds strange. I can hardly believe it myself."

Junius smiled. "That pleases me, Marcus. I know your brother would be pleased that you want to help her and take care of her," he said.

"I hope so," Marcus replied thoughtfully.

The servants began coming in the kitchen for the midday meal. Marcus and Junius could hear the noise from the library. "Come," Junius said. "It's time to share some of our thoughts with them."

The servants acted surprised when Marcus and Junius came in and sat with them at the table in the kitchen. Junius began, "My trusted and faithful servants; as you know, our lives were changed a short time ago when Lucius Marius had his accident. Marcus saw Livia and Rhea yesterday and has come to report that they are doing well in the Marius home. Lucius is gone for the winter and they are in good spirits. There may come a time when it will be necessary to get Livia and Rhea out of his home. If it comes to that, we may be required to pay a high price for our part in it."

He was silent for a few moments to let the idea sink in. He continued, "I want each of you to take until tomorrow and decide if you would like to find work elsewhere." At that remark several of the servants gasped. "If you wish, we will help you find work on other estates. We will give you a good recommendation and you will be safe from what surely is to come."

The mood was somber for the rest of the meal. This was the only home some of them had ever known and they had been treated with kindness and respect. They knew it was not so on many different estates and the thought of leaving there filled them with sadness.

Most of the women had tears in their eyes. As they began to leave the table, Junius said again, "Think on it and pray. God will show you what you should do."

Early the next morning Claudius came in to the main part of the house. He found Junius sitting in his chair with his head bowed in prayer. Claudius cleared his throat. Junius looked up to see his oldest and most trusted servant.

"Master Junius," Claudius said, "We talked about what you said until late into the night. We prayed so that we could be sure that what we decided was the right thing to do.

We have all made a decision to stay. You have been a good and kind master and we have loved your children as if they were our own. We learned to care for Livia and Rhea when they came into this home. You and your family are our family and we will not leave you now. We will stay and pray for you and we will share whatever fate awaits you."

Junius was overcome with emotion. This decision had not been come to lightly. They all had heard of how the Marius family treated their enemies. The stories were legendary and they were all aware of how cruel they could be.

Junius stood and held Claudius by the arm. "Thank you, Claudius. Your loyalty means more to me than I can ever say."

When Marcus came into the room a few moments later he saw tears in his father's eyes. Expecting the worst, he said, "Father, how many of our servants are leaving?"

"None," Junius replied. "They're all going to stay and share our fate, whatever it is."

Marcus was also touched by their selfless devotion. He fell silent and felt encouraged by the support of those he had spent so many years with. Finally, he said, “Father, this is a gift that I hoped for but did not expect.”

“I am encouraged also, Son,” Junius replied. “Let us thank each one of them when they come in for their morning meal. We will pray for wisdom, strength and provision. We will need them all when the time comes.”

Chapter Nineteen

September 312 AD

It had been a few weeks since Livia had last seen Marcus. The men had been working on the servants' quarters and they were looking fresh and clean with the new whitewash on the walls. Mago had grudgingly consented to get new blankets for their beds and had even allowed a few extra pieces of furniture in their rooms. The rooms seemed more comfortable and Livia was pleased with the results.

Mago told her he was seeing a difference in the servants' attitudes. They seemed more contented and they were smiling more. Even the surliest ones seemed to go about their work with a better attitude. They seemed appreciative of Livia and her efforts on their behalf. They treated her with a genuine respect and were beginning to show a care and devotion to her that he had not thought possible.

For herself, Livia was content learning her new role with the help of Mago. The two of them took breakfast in the dining room and talked about the day and any special work that needed to be done. She then returned to the kitchen and praised the servants for the good job they had done the day before. She gave them special instructions for the work they needed to do that day and was careful to include she and Rhea somewhere in the daily projects, so as to build a sense of community in the home

Livia was aware of a new respect coming from Mago. He was seeing what a difference it made to treat the servants with a measure of care and kindness. He was yelling less at each one and was not striking them as often.

She had asked him to stop hitting them entirely but he had not yet complied. This morning she would ask him for another change.

She sat for a few moments, eating, and then said, "Mago, do you think we could give the servants a half day off every week?"

"Whatever for?" he asked.

"I want them to have part of a day to rest and recuperate from their weekly labor. I don't care which day it is, but possibly part of Saturday or Sunday would work well," she replied.

"I'll have to think on it for a while, Mistress Livia. If I'm not careful, you'll be spoiling them and they will all become soft," he said gruffly.

"It's something we did at home, and they seemed to really appreciate it. I think they actually worked better with a day off," she replied.

"You gave them a whole day off?" he asked.

"Yes, it was Junius' idea, and it worked out well," she said.

"Hmmm…" was all Mago said, with a frown on his face.

Livia was not going with him to the market today. It was sprinkling out and she didn't like to go out in the cold, wet weather. Unbeknownst to Mago, she intended to look at each servant's clothing and make sure that they had what they needed to stay warm this winter. The dampness in this home was much greater than that in the country. Ravenna itself had only a sea wall separating it from the Adriatic. The city was surrounded on three sides by water. The fog that rolled in every night made the house much colder. Even with all of the braziers lit, she couldn't get rid of the chill.

She went downstairs and was checking on the women's clothes when Erebes came to find her. "Mistress, your brother is here again."

Livia raised her head with a start. She touched her hair inadvertently to feel if it was in order. "I'll be right there," Livia said. She turned and started for the servants' entrance with a lightness in her step. She could feel her heart racing. She smiled and said, "Marcus, come in. Won't you have some warm wine to take the chill away?"

"I can only stay a short time. I have a lot of deliveries to make today," he answered.

Livia turned to Erebes. "Please have them prepare some bread, cheese and warm wine. We will be upstairs in a few moments." The servant left immediately to follow her instructions.

Marcus looked around to make sure no one else was around. "Livia, we have a plan to get you and Rhea out of here," he whispered.

Livia's eyes grew wide at the thought. "But none of you will be safe if we leave," she said, concern heavy in her voice.

"Sh-h-h," he said as he put his fingers on her lips. He looked her in the eyes and said,

"Father and I have discussed this. He is in agreement that we must get you far away from here. Our thought is to take you both to Carthage. We agreed you would be safe there."

The touch of his hand on her face made her feel warm all over. She looked at him silently and thought for a few moments. She then made her decision. "Yes, we will go; but when and how?" she asked.

"We will go in the spring when it is no longer mare clausum[12]. When the weather clears, ships will begin to travel. We will leave before Lucius comes back, hopefully," he went on to say.

"But the cost...", she started to say.

"After the harvest, there will be enough money," he replied.

They heard a servant coming down the stairs and Marcus took his hand off her face.

"Come, please have something warm to drink and eat," she said casually, as she led him down the hall and up the stairs to the dining room.

She saw Rhea and asked her to sit with Marcus for a few moments, then left and went to her bedroom and got into her chest. She found the inlaid box with the gold aurei from her dowry. She took the key from her secret hiding place in her drawer and opened the box. It was all there - enough to purchase three tickets on a ship and perhaps some extra for living expenses in Carthage.

Marcus was sitting with Rhea in the dining room when Livia walked in carrying the box. Rhea knew what was in the box and her eyes widened. Marcus had no idea, and just looked at the box inquisitively.

Livia looked around to see if anyone was near. "The lock is broken on this box and I need you to take it and get it fixed for me," she said, as she gave him the box and the key.

Marcus lifted the box and felt the weight of it. He knew what it probably had in it.

"Use all of this as you need to," she whispered. "It was my dowry when I married Stephanas and he returned it to

---

[12] meaning closed sea, ships did not travel between November 12th and the 10th of March

me before he passed. He thought I might have a use for it someday. Little did he know it would be used in circumstances like these." Marcus looked at the box and became thoughtful. "Livia…," he began.

"You are all risking so much; let me also share in this way," she said as quietly as she could.

Marcus finished the bread, cheese and warm wine in silence. He rose to go and took the box in his hands. "I will get the lock fixed on it and will gladly return it to you," he said, in case anyone was listening.

Livia led him down the hall and the stairs to the servants' entrance. She opened the door and looked at him wistfully. "I wish you didn't have to go so soon."

"I will come again when I can," he said. He took his hand and placed it over hers on the door handle. "Thank you," he said, as he looked at the box.

"Marcus, we will pray - we will pray that this will all work out," she whispered as he went out the door. She watched him enter the boat and look back. He waved and she raised her hand to signal goodbye.

She closed the door and walked slowly back to the servants' quarters. Her mind was full of hope, dread and fear. All she could think of was, "What if? What if we can get away?" She began to feel hopeful. A few moments later it was followed by, "What if we are caught; what will happen to us?" She then began to feel fear. Her fear was not as great as her dread, though. "What if Lucius returns and takes me to his bed?"

That was the worst thought and the one she had been thinking about every day while he was gone to Rome. She truly dreaded what would happen to her when he returned.

This had to be the answer they were all praying for. She had lain in her bed night after night wondering what she would do when he finally approached her with what he really wanted from her. How would she respond? Would she need to give him her body in order to protect her family?

She had a sense of relief that this is what Marcus and Junius had decided to do. She and Rhea would be taken out of here before it was too late. They would pray that the weather would cooperate and they could leave in early March before Lucius returned.

She couldn't keep her mind on her work and so she went upstairs to find Rhea.

"Could you help me in my room, please?" she asked her.

Rhea followed her into her room and shut the door. "Mistress Livia, what is happening and why did you give Master Marcus your dowry?" she asked quietly.

Livia told her the plans to go to Carthage. Rhea's eyes grew wider and wider. "Can it really be true? Is there a way out of here for us?" she wondered.

"If the Lord wills, we will only have to spend the winter here," Livia answered.

"But what of Lucius? He will be so angry when he finds out you are gone. Will he come looking for us? Can he have us arrested?" she asked.

"I don't think so," Livia said slowly as she thought about the question. "We won't have broken any laws or agreements. He wanted me to come and run his household and work with his servants. I will have done that. He didn't specify a time frame. He and I both knew I wasn't coming forever - just for a time - mostly just for as long as he wanted me here, if you know what I mean."

"I do," Rhea said grimly, "and that is what I have been concerned about night and day."

"We will pray, Rhea, and we will hope," Livia said wistfully. She turned to leave the bedroom with a renewed sense of purpose. "Let us do our best here so that when we are gone, there will be evidence that while we were here, we were a credit to the Lord."

Rhea followed her out the door and closed it. "I, too, will pray and hope, and I will work hard; for the Lord, for you and for all those in this home."

Livia turned and looked at Rhea. Her eyes were moist from the emotion she felt.

She hugged her and said, "Thank you, Rhea, thank you.

Chapter Twenty

Marcus left the Marius home in a state of wonder. He looked at the box and set it in the bow of the boat. He covered it with ropes and an oiled tarp so that it would not be noticed during the rest of his deliveries. He returned to the shop in the late afternoon and took the box to a private section of the warehouse. He turned the key in the lock and opened the lid. He gasped as he saw its contents. It was filled with gold aurei - enough to buy them passage to Carthage. He realized he had been holding his breath, and he let the air out of his lungs slowly. There was more than enough here for the trip. He hoped they would have money enough to rent a small home and perhaps open a small business when they got there.

Marcus was amazed that their needs had been supplied so quickly. It made him feel that he and Junius were on the right track in deciding that they should leave. If he had doubted for a second that the plan was not the right thing to do, this surprising provision took away any doubt.

The thought of Livia warmed his heart. He was pleased she had consented to go so quickly. He had not asked her to marry him, but she must know that was what he had in mind. It was too soon to talk of marriage, but it was all but settled in his mind.

Tomorrow, if his uncle consented, he would go to the port in Classis.[13] There would be some ships there, and he would see if he could find out how much it would cost them to get passage for Carthage.

---

[13] Ravenna's main port situated a few miles south of the city. Historically it had been an important port for the Roman navy.

Marcus needed to talk to his uncle. He hadn't told him what they had planned to do, because he didn't want to involve him. His father had told him to share their plans with Rufus. He could be trusted and he also needed to have the freedom to disassociate himself with Marcus if he chose to. Marcus put the box in a safe place. He would retrieve it when he had finished talking with his uncle.

Marcus found his uncle closing the warehouse for the day. "Uncle, could I talk to you privately for a few moments before going home?"

Rufus signaled to his servant to go home and turned to Marcus. "Marcus, I also wanted to talk to you and let you know what I heard today."

Marcus looked at his uncle and decided to put his news aside for the moment.

"What is it, Uncle?" he queried.

"I have news that the Emperor Constantine has conquered Verona and is heading south. If he takes the coast road, the officials of Ravenna are going to go out and meet him and welcome him into the city. They are betting on the fact that if he could beat Maxentius's forces in Verona, he will be able to conquer any other city in northern Italia.

No one wants a fight with his army and I for one am thankful that there will be peace in our region."

Marcus stared at his uncle. His own plans paled in comparison to what was going on in the north. Should he even share his news now? Marcus waited for a few moments. His uncle saw his hesitation and said, "What is it, Son? What did you want to talk about?"

He looked at his uncle and took a deep breath. "As you know, Livia is staying at the home of Lucius Marius. I have spoken to her today about leaving there in the spring."

Rufus's eyebrows went up, and he waited.

"Uncle, I want to take her to Carthage, where she would be out of his reach."

Rufus looked surprised, "Carthage - must you take her to another country?"

"She needs to be far enough away from Lucius so that he can't find her and bring her back," Marcus explained.

"But Carthage; isn't there somewhere closer you could go? Does your father know of your plan?" Rufus asked.

"Yes," Marcus replied. "He approves of the plan, but he knows that it could be costly for you once we are gone. I had planned to seek employment elsewhere because I wanted to distance myself from you and your family when the time came."

Rufus remained thoughtful. After a few moments he said, "What can Lucius Marius do to us? We won't have broken any laws."

"That's true, but he could try to destroy your business. He's a powerful man and is known to retaliate against any who try to cross him," Marcus said.

"Yes, he has that reputation, but I will take my chances. I would do anything to help you and Junius. If he approves of this plan, then I will do whatever I need to in order to help," Rufus said.

Marcus could hear the conviction in his voice. It gave him courage to speak. "If I stay with you, I will be able to keep in touch with her without anyone suspecting anything," Marcus said.

Rufus continued to be pensive. He let out a deep sigh and his shoulders sagged, "Your father just lost one son, and soon he will be losing another. I feel like I will be losing a son also."

Marcus began to feel a sense of loss also. "I'm not happy about it, Uncle Rufus. I don't want to leave everything I know and live in a foreign country, but I don't know any other way to get Livia completely away from him," Marcus said. "With your permission, I wanted to go to the port in Classis tomorrow and find out how much it will cost to buy passage for the three of us to Carthage."

"I'm sure it will be steep. Go - it will be our secret. No one must know; none of the workers here, and especially none of the women at home. You know that the women have never been able to keep a secret. If this is going to work, we must keep our own counsel," Rufus remarked.

"Thank you, Uncle Rufus, I am indebted to you." Marcus turned away from him feeling a myriad of emotions. He was thankful his uncle was supportive of him, but the thought of leaving him and the business caused a tightness in his stomach. He retrieved the inlaid box and he and Rufus walked home together.

Marcus went straight to his room and found a place to hide the box. He was quiet during dinner and returned to his room to think. He knew there was one thing he must settle before he went to the port the next morning.

Marcus knew that the decision to take Livia away would change his life forever. He was not afraid to marry her, but the thought of fleeing from such a powerful man gave him pause. They could be in danger from the moment he took her away from Lucius's house. Was he truly prepared to face any consequences that might happen to them? Marcus knew in his heart that he wasn't. The thought of just relying on himself for protection gave him no peace whatsoever. Marcus knew he needed someone bigger than himself to rely on.

Marcus slowly got down on his knees by his bed. He didn't quite know where to begin. He thought for a while and then spoke quietly; "Lord, I know I have been running from you for years. I have been living my life for myself and I haven't wanted anything to do with you. I know I've offended you greatly and I ask your forgiveness for going my own way and doing whatever I wanted. I give myself to you from this night forward and I promise to follow you for the rest of my life." Marcus stayed on his knees for a while longer. He wanted the Lord to know he was serious about what he had said and that he was making a pact with him.

As Marcus rose, he felt as if a gigantic load had been lifted off of his shoulders. A quiet peace began to envelop him. He knew he had been heard and that God had accepted his confession. The turmoil that Marcus had lived with for years began to lessen as the peace spread through his being. Marcus stayed awake long after the sun had set and thought about the future. He knew that if the Lord were watching out for them, he could face anything that would come their way. With those thoughts in mind, he drifted off to sleep and slept better than he had in years.

The next morning Marcus woke with a renewed sense of purpose and set out for the port at Classis. It was a short distance south of the city, and as he approached the port, he could see four ships docked there. The largest was a Roman galley. He wanted to avoid anything that was associated with the government and so he steered clear of that one. He would go to each of the smaller ships to see which might be going south to Carthage, and he would be able to get a reasonable idea of what it was going to cost them to make the journey.

He spoke to a man working on the dock alongside the first ship. The man said it was going east across the Adriatic to Nicomedia. As he got closer to the second ship, he noticed that it had the lines of an Egyptian ship. The man in charge told him it was leaving for Alexandria in the morning. He pointed to the last ship, "The Bonum Fortuna[14] will eventually leave for Carthage. I don't know when it will be ready to sail."

The Bonum Fortuna looked like a hive of activity. As he neared, he noticed men sawing away at burned timbers near the top of the hull. One of the men on the wharf told him that a fire had started in the cooking area and had damaged part of the interior of the ship, spreading to the hull. He said the repairs were not going well as they were not able to get the timbers they needed to fix the damage quickly.

Marcus asked the man where the ship was headed. The man told him they were going south to Brundisium[15] and then on to Carthage, but that they might be stuck here through the winter. Marcus's ears perked up at this news. Marcus asked where the captain might be and was directed to a tavern a short distance away from the dock.

Marcus quickly walked there and found the captain eating prandium, the midday meal, by himself. He introduced himself and asked if he could speak with him a moment. He told him he needed to go to Carthage and asked what the cost would be to take three people there.

"Would you be staying on deck in a tent?" the captain asked Marcus thought for a moment. He knew it would be much cheaper to stay on deck, but the idea of Livia and Rhea in a tent on the deck during inclement weather did not

---

[14] Good Fortune

[15] A major Roman port in southern Italia, modern day Brindisi

sound appealing to him. "Do you have any berths for passengers?"

"The ship has several berths for passengers. I have a small one that three people could stay in for the right price," the captain said smiling. Marcus thought he saw the glint of avarice in his eyes.

"What would be the cost for that one?" Marcus asked.

When the captain told Marcus the price, he fought his emotions in order not to wince. The money Livia had given him would cover the cost, but would not leave them as much as he had hoped to begin their new life with. "My wife and I do not plan to leave until the spring."

"I don't know if we will be able to leave here before then, either, the work is not going as fast as I hoped it would. Come back in a month. If I am still in port, we will talk further."

As Marcus turned to leave, the enormity of what he was planning hit him. The trip was going to cost them a great deal - their homes, their family, their friends and a lot of their money. They were going to literally have to say good-bye to everything and everyone they had known. He walked slowly away from the tavern, feeling the impact of what they were planning.

His resolve wavered for a few minutes as he walked back to his horse. Was this what he really wanted to do? Of course, he didn't want to do it, but he could see no other way out of the situation. Did he feel ready to take on a wife and a new life? No, he didn't, but he felt he must do it for Livia's sake. He straightened his back, raised his head up and prayed silently, "Lord, help me. I can't do this without you."

Chapter Twenty-one

October 312 A.D.

Lucius Marius slowly changed into the rough tunic he had borrowed from one of his servants. He was awaiting a farm wagon that would take him out of the city. His mind went to the purpose for this ruse. He had been summoned to the Curia[16] last evening by his father and a few of the most influential senators. They had a message for him to deliver to the Emperor Constantine.

Constantine had, since September, been able to dominate northern and central Italia and was now camped several miles outside Rome. He had arrived a few days ago and the news had brought unrest in the city. Rome's enemies had laid siege to the city in the past, and the populace knew how hard a siege could be on everyone.

Since Lucius had met Constantine in Mediolanum, he was the perfect one to take the senators' message to him. Yes, there would be dire consequences should Lucius and the senators be found out, but they were willing to risk it. The Emperor Maxentius could be brutal when crossed; and taking a treasonous message to Constantine would result in death for all involved, if they were caught.

His father's small group had made all of the arrangements. Getting to Constantine's army took some planning as Maxentius had cut all but one of the bridges across the Tiber River. He hoped to keep the invading army from crossing them and entering Rome. Fortunately, Senator Gallicus had property that bordered the Tiber not far from where Constantine's army was encamped. Lucius

[16] The Curia Hostilia was the building the Senate met in. It is situated in the northwest corner of the Forum.

would be taken to the property and would be forded across the river. Word had already been sent to Constantine that a representative from the Senate would be seeing him this evening. He agreed to have a soldier and an extra horse waiting on the other side of the river in order to bring the representative to him.

Lucius began to sweat and the rough cloth made his skin itch. Even though clean, it didn't smell like his clothing. He looked at the cloak he would wear. It was rough also, but the hood would keep him from being recognized as he traveled through the city. Just then, a servant came to announce that there was a man at the rear entrance of the house waiting for him.

Lucius got up on the wagon and sat on the seat next to the driver. He said nothing to the man as they made their way through the city. As they approached the gate, Lucius pulled his hood down covering his face. They were just one of a multitude of wagons leaving Rome this afternoon. They were all empty of their produce, as the populace were stocking up in preparation for the coming siege. The driver of the cart looked up at the soldiers and was waved through the gate. Thankfully, nothing looked out of the ordinary. Lucius breathed a sigh of relief as they left the city.

The road was full of traffic as they headed north. Many citizens were leaving the city, in anticipation of the coming siege. Lucius kept his thoughts to himself as they passed many on foot carrying their belongings. He kept the hood over his face in an effort not to be recognized by anyone. He didn't want to be seen leaving the city like this. He didn't want anyone to know about his treacherous behavior.

They made the eight mile trip in just a few hours. The driver dropped Lucius off at the rear entrance of the house.

He knocked on the door and was greeted by Castor, the eldest son of Senator Gallicus. He lifted the bag with his toga, shoes and cloak in it. He would dress for his meeting with Constantine and soon deliver the message orally. Nothing had been written down in case he was discovered.

Lucius had met Castor before, but they didn't speak much; the less said the better. He was taken to a room where he could bathe and dress. There was a platter with food and a bottle of wine waiting for him. Lucius washed his hands and face. He was famished and decided to eat first before he readied himself. He ate slowly and thought about the coming meeting with Constantine as he drank his wine. He was in no hurry to dress as he wouldn't leave before dark. The sun hadn't set yet so it would be at least an hour before he would be under cover of darkness.

Lucius bathed, dressed and walked to the window. It was dark now and he would soon be going. He was relieved when he heard the knock at the door. His stomach felt nervous as he turned to go out the door. He was led out of the house and across a field to the river. A small boat was waiting and he took a deep breath to calm himself as he entered it. Once he crossed the river and met Constantine's soldier, there would be no turning back. He knew his actions were treasonous, but he had made his choice, and he was prepared to live with the consequences.

As planned, one of Constantine's soldiers was waiting for them on the other side of the river. He greeted him and gave Lucius the reins to a horse. Lucius mounted the horse and began the final mile to Constantine's camp. As he approached it, he was surprised at the size of it. He could see small warming fires burning over a vast area. He began to feel confident that he had made the right decision to come and that he would soon be on the winning side. The soldier took him within about twenty feet of Constantine's tent. He let the guard know who he had with him and Lucius got off of the horse and waited. He stood straight and tall, and tried to look as confident as he could. He was not here to cower or to beg; he was here to offer this invader the city itself.

A general came out of Constantine's tent towards him, "The Emperor will see you now." Lucius walked towards him and followed him into the tent. He saw Constantine seated in front of a table with a map on it. Constantine rolled the map up and raised his head. He immediately recognized Lucius Marius.

"Lucius, come, sit and have a glass of wine," Constantine said.

Lucius looked at the other men seated in the room. Should he ask to speak to Constantine alone or should he give the senators' message in the hearing of others? In a split second he decided to say what he had come for in the presence of all in the tent.

He took his seat and waited for the wine to be poured. He would follow protocol and not speak until the Emperor spoke to him.

"So, Lucius Marius, what news have you brought me from the Senate?" Constantine asked.

Lucius knew him to be a man of action who did not appreciate the normal pleasantries of court banter. He started slowly, wanting to get the message across clearly.

"Your Highness, this message is not from the full Senate, but from several influential senators. They wish for you to know that they will ally themselves with you and your cause. At the moment, Maxentius is acting as if nothing is wrong and you are not a threat to the city. Our sources tell us that he is now hoping to use the Fabian tactics from the past and keep the gates of Rome closed. He is sure that, as in the case of Hannibal, your army will begin to starve, and you will leave.

“That is what we expected,” Constantine said, “and we have stocked up and are prepared for a long siege.”

“Our desire is to help you from the inside of the city,” Lucius began. “We desire to work against Maxentius on all levels. First, we will have the landowners put pressure on him not to burn their fields. We will plant rumors around the city that you are invincible and have men begin to stir up the rabble. We don’t believe it will take much to get the people to riot in favor of you.”

“It will take more than that to defeat Maxentius; he is safe as long as he stays within your city walls,” Constantine said.

“Yes, that is our next point,” Lucius said. “One of the senators is one of his closest advisors. He believes he could pressure Maxentius to bring his army out of the gates to engage you in battle once the tide of popularity begins to turn against him. He knows others in the Emperor’s inner circle who could be bribed to exert pressure on him also.

“That would shorten our work here considerably,” Constantine said appreciatively.

After a moment, he continued, “And what would these august senators want in return for such help?”

Lucius, not wanting to lose his momentum said, “They want the power of the Senate restored to it.”

Constantine’s face showed surprise. He hesitated and then smiled. “Tell them that I shall reward my friends and allies when this campaign comes to a successful conclusion.” They both looked at each other for a moment and Constantine decided the interview was over. “Thank you for coming, Lucius Marius. I look forward to seeing you next when I am within the gates of Rome."

Lucius turned to go. As he left the tent, he saw the soldier who had brought him waiting with the horses. Lucius got on his mount and followed the soldier back to the river where he would cross in the awaiting boat. He couldn't help smiling in the dark. No one could see him, but he knew that the meeting had gone well. He was glad he had been chosen to go; perhaps he would even benefit from this in time. They reached the Tiber and he was taken across the river. He then followed the servant back to the house where he was again greeted by Castor. This time, however, Castor looked at him intently. Lucius looked at him, nodded and then smiled. Castor said nothing but smiled in return. He was taken to his room where he took off his toga, and then laid down to rest. The wagon would not be leaving for the city until a few hours before dawn. Lucius tried to rest but his mind kept playing over his meeting with Constantine. Finally, his mind relaxed, as did his body and he dozed off.

He had only been asleep a short time when he heard a knock at the door. He was again led to the back of the house and the awaiting wagon. He turned to Castor and they looked at each other. Castor was in this as deep as he was and an understanding passed between them. He took Castor's arm and clasped it. He turned and went out the door.

He looked at the wagon he had ridden in. This morning it was laden with produce from the fields. He put the cloak on to keep warm and sat down. In a few hours he would be back in the city and make a full report to his father and the other senators. With any luck from the gods, they would have a new emperor within a few weeks. That thought alone made him almost giddy as he settled in for the trip back to Rome.

Chapter Twenty-two

October 28, 312

Lucius Marius stood on the steps of the Curia next to his father. The senators watched as Maxentius rode past in full battle array. He was leading his Praetorians and part of the Italian army out of the city. They were headed to the plain of Saxa Ruba in order to engage Constantine's forces.

Lucius just shook his head in wonder. It had taken about a week after he returned for the rabble to be stirred up and the riots to start. Men had been paid handsomely to proclaim that Constantine was invincible because he was a god. Others had been paid to get the multitude to demand Maxentius go out and meet the invading army. The pressure began to mount on Maxentius to answer the people with a solution.

Thanks to more of the senators' money, most of his advisors were telling him he must go out and meet Constantine on the battlefield. Keeping the gates of Rome closed was not a feasible alternative. The farmers had mutinied against him and refused to burn their fields. Hence, the invaders were eating well off the land. It seemed like everywhere he turned, the tide had turned against him.

Becoming more and more desperate to save face, Maxentius approached those that held the Sybillene books. He found that an ancient oracle had declared that the enemy of Rome would be killed on the 28th of October. Even though the prophecy was vague, he had it proclaimed publicly. He would go out of the city gates in order to fight the invader. So today, the 28th of October, he was marching out to defend Rome from Constantine.

Lucius would leave in a few hours in order to find out what the disposition of the battle would be. There would be no need to rush. It would take a few hours for the army to march the nine miles to the plain of Saxa Ruba. Somehow, they must cross the Tiber near the Milvian Bridge. Lucius decided he would stay on this side of the river, and not venture near the battlefield. Soon enough, he hoped, Rome would have a new emperor.

As the day wore on, Lucius mounted his horse and left Rome. The closer he got to the site of the battle, the more he saw people on the road fleeing in the direction of Rome. No one, it seemed, wanted to be caught in the middle between two armies. He couldn't go as fast as he wanted to and he cursed the fates as his progress was slowed by those going the other way. It was well past noon and he was still a few miles away from the battle. As he neared the area, he was met by soldiers from the Italian army fleeing towards Rome. He stopped one and asked what had happened. "We were routed, Sir, and what's worse, the Emperor has fallen into the river and drowned."

"If it were only true," Lucius thought to himself. "Tell me exactly what happened." The soldier looked him up and down before answering. He saw the purple stripe on the edge of his toga and that was enough to let him know he was speaking to someone in an official capacity. "Their cavalry charged and broke through our armored cavalry. The infantry attacked and we were driven back. As we were retreating, across the bridge."

"What bridge?" Lucius interrupted him.

"The pontoon bridge we constructed this morning. That's how the army crossed this morning. We fought with our back to the Tiber in case we had to retreat. We were retreating and the Emperor started across the bridge. His horse reared and he fell into the river. Several troops jumped in the river after him, but he sank with his armor on and the river took him down stream. We were not able to find him." The soldier looked distraught as he finished speaking.

"An ill omen indeed," was all Lucius would say. He would not feign concern for Maxentius at this point. "I must see what is happening for myself."

Lucius continued on and as he neared the river, he urged his horse up a small hill to get a better view of what was happening. What he saw shocked and saddened him. On the plain he could see the Praetorians fighting for all they were worth. They appeared to be outnumbered, but were holding their ground.

For years he had hated the Praetorians. They held the real power in Rome. It was they who kept the emperors in power, and it was at their whim that an emperor rose or fell. They knew they held the power, and that knowledge had created an arrogance and disdain for everyone, regardless of rank or social standing. The Praetorians had been the protectors of Rome and Lucius knew they would die in an effort to protect the city from the invading army.

He watched them fall for about half an hour. He could not take seeing those brave men die in the face of overwhelming odds. Truly, he was seeing courage at its finest.

He never thought he would be sad to see the Praetorians beaten, but the sight created a sorrow he had not thought possible. Knowing the outcome of the battle, he turned his horse around and headed back to Rome.

A few hours later he returned to the Senate and told them what he had seen. They would have a new emperor by tonight. After his report, they began to talk among themselves about what kind of leader Constantine would be. Having done his duty for the day, Lucius asked to be excused and returned to his house.

He ate his dinner and had a few glasses of wine. What he had seen today had shaken him. True, he had never seen an actual battle take place, but he didn't believe it was that.

He had seen men die to protect him and those in the city, and it spoke volumes to him.

Would he die to protect others? He doubted it. He had always been one to seek his own self-interests, and he wanted nothing to do with self-sacrifice.

He lay down, but sleep wouldn't come. The battle scene kept playing out in front of his eyes. He knew he had been part of the downfall of these brave men, and he began to feel an overwhelming guilt. What had he done? He had been in on the plot to overthrow

Maxentius from the beginning. Surely, he knew men were going to die, but to see them do it, and do it so bravely, made him ashamed to his very core. He tossed and turned for hours until he fell asleep from exhaustion.

The next morning, he awoke bleary-eyed and dressed. He must be at the Curia today; surely Constantine would be arriving in Rome to declare his victory to the people. It seemed a hollow victory to Lucius now, but he must be there alongside the senators to welcome him.

For the second day in a row he watched an emperor ride before the senators at the head of his army. He stood next to his father as he had done the day before. His father was smiling for all he was worth and was waiting for Constantine to ascend the steps of the Temple of Jupiter and offer a libation to the gods. What happened next shocked Lucius as well as the people watching the spectacle.

Constantine did not get off his horse and ascend the steps, but ignored the priest waiting to help him with his libation. The Senate and the people took immediate offence at his action. At that point Lucius looked at his army as they continued on to the Forum. They had a strange symbol on their shields. Surely this had some significance. He had not seen the mark on their shields when he went for his clandestine meeting a few days before.

Lucius watched as Constantine stopped near the Senate. Many senators greeted him in the midst of their consternation. The people cheered half-heartedly as they too, were unsure what to do at this breach of custom. It was obvious no one knew what to think of their new emperor. The festivities went on until he left for his Imperial residence.

The next day Constantine went to the Curia in order to address the Senate. Lucius listened as the Senate congratulated him on his victory. At that point, Lucius slipped away from the proceedings in order to find out what the symbol meant. He left the chamber and found a ranking officer. He had seen him the night he had gone to Constantine's tent. "Centurion, what is the meaning of the symbol on your shields?" The man looked around and then took Lucius aside in order to speak to him quietly.

"A few days ago, we saw a shining cross in the sky. That night the Emperor had a dream in which a man told him to conquer in this sign. His advisors told him the man was Jesus Christ and so the next day we were ordered to carve this symbol into our shields."

Lucius tried not to let the shock register on his face. He had noticed the shields from a distance yesterday, but could not clearly make out what was on them. "Has the Emperor in fact become a Christian?" Lucius asked, hoping it was not true.

"I don't know, but he seems to be leaning in the direction of the Christian god," the officer replied.

Lucius thanked him for the information and turned to walk back to the chamber. His family had been repulsed by the Christians from the beginning. It was a bloody religion that started with the death of their leader by crucifixion. That was nothing he or his father wanted any part of. Lucius was sure that the senators had not bargained for this when they had sent him out to meet with Constantine.

The Emperor Maxentius had no morals and had offended the populace with his outrageous behavior. Now, would they suffer from just the opposite? Had Constantine truly joined the Christian cult - one that denied the Roman gods? Would he follow a religion that denied the carnal pleasures of this life and lived for some future kingdom? Worse yet, would he try to force all of them to his new found religion? Lucius dismissed the last thought. The people would never stand for it, thank the gods. And speaking of the gods, how could they let this happen to their beloved Rome?

Chapter Twenty-three

It was nearing the end of December; much had changed politically in the empire since Livia and Rhea had come to live in the Marius home. There was the new Emperor Constantine; Livia and Rhea had heard much talk in the market place about him. Many had heard that he was a Christian; Livia hoped so. Perhaps a time would come when Christians could worship without fear again. In spite of all the changes in the empire, her life was still the same. She wasn't complaining though, her time in the Marius home had been somewhat pleasant.

Today was a holiday for the Roman people. It was the first day of the Feast of Saturnalia. It occurred during the winter solstice and it was a time of giving gifts to the servants. The servants looked forward to it and traditionally had the day off. If they were fortunate, the householders would serve them for a change. From what Livia and Rhea had gathered from the servants, it hadn't been celebrated in the Marius house for many years.

Livia decided, with Mago's permission, of course, that this year would be different. The servants were told that they would be celebrating it this year, and that each one would have the entire day off. Every servant in the Marius home was looking forward to it. They had not received anything in the way of gifts for years, but the thought of a whole day off sounded luxurious to them.

As Christians, Livia and Rhea did not celebrate this festival, but they knew that the servants desired to, and so it became important to them. Livia wanted to do something special for each one, as she had come to care about them deeply. At the beginning of November, she began to think about what they could do to make their day special.

Mago had grudgingly allowed warmer tunics to be purchased for each servant and she and Rhea had sewn a border on each one. The women's tunics had a border of flowers on the hem and the mens' tunics had a masculine design sewn around the neck. She and Rhea had worked on them in their rooms at night in order to make them a surprise.

After she knew that she was leaving and would not be able to take all of her things with her, she talked to Rhea about giving the women a present out of the clothing they had brought with them. Together they had enough clothing to give each woman an extra tunic. She had also purchased extra wool and she and Rhea had made a new woolen cloak for each man, including Mago. She could hardly wait to give the gifts to them.

She and Rhea had risen earlier than usual this morning in order to get breakfast ready for the household. As they worked, there was an air of anticipation in the kitchen. The servants began coming in the kitchen for their breakfast. They knew they would be celebrating the holiday, but they didn't know what to expect. They were surprised to see Livia and Rhea preparing the morning meal. They began serving each one as they took their place around the table. Livia waited for all of them to arrive before she spoke to them.

"Today Rhea and I will be preparing the meals for each one of you. You will also have the entire day off," she began. The servants quickly looked to Mago to see if he had approved. He just nodded. They began to smile and laugh. "That is not all. You have all worked so hard these past few months, we have gifts for each of you."

Livia and Rhea had placed the presents behind the kitchen door that morning. Each one was folded neatly. As they began to distribute them, many of the servants gasped.

There was a look of wonder on their faces for they had not experienced this level of kindness for years. Livia wanted them to know the gifts were not just from her.

"These gifts are from Master Lucius, Mago, Rhea and myself," she explained.

Master Lucius paid for the new tunics and the material for the cloaks. Mago approved the purchases and Rhea and I sewed the borders on them. We want you to know how much we appreciate each one of you."

A few of the women had tears in their eyes as they looked at their presents. The men were very quiet and a few were gulping their emotions down. She turned to Mago and gave him a new woolen cloak also. She had embroidered a beautiful design on the border.

He seemed taken aback by her kindness to him.

She looked at Mago and said, "You have been considerate of me since the first day we arrived and I thank you for it," she said.

"You and Rhea have been a welcome addition to this household." Mago replied with sincerity.

The servants nodded their heads in agreement. They ate their breakfast in a lighthearted mood. "The day is yours to do with as you wish," Livia said. "We will serve you lunch and dinner at the usual time."

She and Rhea cleaned up the kitchen and began to talk about what they would prepare for lunch. Mago came back into the kitchen and said, "Mistress Livia, that was truly a kind thing you and Rhea did for each one of us."

"Each of you need to know how important you are in our eyes," she replied.

"You truly have worked wonders around here," he stated.

"It is amazing how a little kindness can change many things," she said. Perhaps he would see that yelling at the servants and striking them was not the answer to getting the best results from them.

"Your methods are unconventional but they have certainly produced the desired effect," he continued. "I was concerned that they would become soft and unruly under your kind hand, but they work harder than they ever did and have a much better attitude."

"Then I have done the job I was brought here to do," she said.

"Yes, indeed you have," he replied appreciatively.

Mago left the room and Livia became thoughtful. She had come to care about each one of the servants and would miss them when she left. Mago had taught her much about running a house in the city. When she had lived on the farm, they had grown practically everything they needed and had bought little. In the city, they had purchased almost everything and one had to learn where and how to shop for the best quality at the best prices. Indeed, she had received quite an education in the last few months.

She realized she would be sad to leave this place. The thought took her by surprise. Here, she truly was the mistress of the house and had earned the respect and affection of total strangers. If only Lucius Marius would not return; she would have been willing to live here with Rhea for the rest of her life. She didn't want to go to Carthage and have to make the adjustments it would take to make a new life there.

Her reverie was broken by Cora and Clio, Argia's daughters. They were wearing their new tunics and they were glowing. “Thank you so much, Mistress Livia and Rhea. We haven’t received presents since the master’s wife was alive, and that was over ten years ago. The border you sewed on them is beautiful,” Clio said.

Livia turned and gave each one of them a hug. “I so appreciate you both and your mother. Your cooking is wonderful; I have never tasted better. I appreciate all of your hard work on behalf of each member of this household.”

They were embarrassed by so much praise and left smiling. The other servants trickled in and out of the kitchen during the morning to thank them also. They in turn received the gift of sincere praise for their efforts on behalf of the household.

Rhea and Livia kept looking at each other after each one left. They knew that the kindness they had bestowed had ultimately come from Christ. They also knew that if it wasn’t for Him they would not be doing so well in this situation. He had surely blessed them and shown them favor here. They would love to share what they knew of Him with each one, but they knew they couldn’t, and it saddened them. They talked of it often when they were by themselves in their rooms.

The day continued on and it was one that brought all of the household closer together. Although the festival continued for a few more days, it would be business as usual tomorrow. Still, Livia cherished this day in her heart. It had been one of joy and mirth in a house that had known little of it. By nightfall she was exhausted but she had an overwhelming sense of peace and joy. She would truly remember this day for many years to come.

Chapter Twenty-Four

January 313 A.D.

Lucius took the last step of the Curia and entered the building. His cloak was wet from the warm rain this January morning. His presence had been requested by the Senate, and he would be given his next assignment. He usually met with his father and a few senators privately who gave him his instructions. As he walked to the small anteroom where they met, he wondered where he would be going next. He tried to swallow his disappointment at the events that had transpired in the past few months since Constantine had entered Rome and become Emperor of the western half of the empire.

His sandals left water on the marble as he walked to the anteroom. As he entered, he was surprised to see that only his father was waiting to talk to him. "Are we waiting for the others?" he queried.

"No, the others are meeting with the full Senate as the Emperor Constantine is addressing them today," his father answered.

Lucius noticed that his father looked tired this morning. He could see his father's nearly sixty years showing on his face; perhaps he hadn't slept well last night. "What is the pleasure of the Senate, Father?" Lucius asked.

"Make ready for a trip to Mediolanum. You will be leaving within the week and will travel with the Emperor's retinue. He informed the Senate this morning that he has every intention of issuing an edict to fully recognize Christianity as a legal religion of the state. He plans to return all property to the church that was confiscated during the last ten years of persecution," his father said.

Lucius looked around the room to make sure the door was shut and there was no chance of being heard. He for one had not minded the persecutions and he knew his father felt the same way. He lowered his voice, "That will give the churches more power and will legitimize them in the people's eyes."

"Yes," was all his father would say.

Lucius whispered now, "There have been some disappointing consequences to the regime change."

His father spoke quietly also, "There's not a citizen in the city of Rome who is not disappointed that Constantine won't make his capital here. Taking the seat of power north and ruling from Mediolanum has been the worst of it. The Roman Empire should be ruled from Rome. That fact should be evident to all involved."

"I never thought I would be disappointed to see the Praetorian guard disbanded, but they did have their place," Lucius whispered.

"Yes, emperors rose and fell at their discretion," his father replied quietly.

"You're right there," Lucius agreed half-heartedly. Lucius was having a difficult time adjusting to all of the changes that had taken place since Constantine had come to power. Up to this point he had not seen anything that had benefited him since Maxentius had been replaced.

"Still the Senate must be pleased with our new ruler," Lucius spoke in a normal tone after a few moments of silence.

"He has more than kept his word. He has given the Senate its rightful place in ruling the people and he is taking a few of us north to be among his advisors in court," his father said smiling.

"You're going north to live?" Lucius asked surprised.

"Yes, and I was hoping I would be welcome in your home," his father said.

"Of course, Father, but why am I going north?" Lucius asked.

"The Senate needs you to bring a signed copy of the new edict back to them. In the meantime, they will be working on the laws that will help the cities and provinces return the church's property back to them," his father explained.

"I am surprised that he doesn't sign it while he is here," Lucius said.

"His hope is that it will not just be for the western half of the empire. Licinius, one of the two rulers of the eastern half of the empire, has agreed to come to Mediolanum and sign the decree. I doubt that he would be happy coming all of the way to Rome in order to benefit the Christians," his father said.

"You're probably right," Lucius answered. "The rulers of the eastern half were the real persecutors of the church. I'm surprised Licinius agreed to come. What of the other ruler of the east, Maximin Daia? Is he coming also?"

"Not a chance. He can't be too happy that the Senate proclaimed Constantine the supreme Augustus of the three. He's probably seething at the moment. He was known for his overwhelming hatred of the Christians," his father said smiling.

"You're really enjoying this aren't you?" Lucius asked.

"And why shouldn't I? The change has benefited our family, and I am sure at some point you will reap some of the benefits also," his father said.

Lucius had always hoped to become an Imperial Legate. He relished the idea of traveling for the Emperor instead of the Senate. He wanted to be as close to the seat of power as possible. He thought about it for a moment and smiled. Perhaps this wouldn't work out too badly for him also. He would not speak of it now to his father. He changed the subject intentionally. "We're fortunate the weather has been so warm this January. It shouldn't make travel too difficult."

"My sentiments exactly. These bones don't do well in the cool, humid weather of Rome. I don't know how they'll do on the road or in the cold of Mediolanum, for that matter," his father said.

"My home is well heated, with few drafts. You will be quite comfortable there; I am sure," Lucius replied. "How long do you think I will be there before returning to Rome?"

"The Emperor hopes to have it signed by mid-February. He wants action on the matter, and he wants it done as soon as possible," his father said.

"When do we leave, Father?" Lucius asked.

"Within the week," his father replied.

Having nothing else to discuss at the moment, Lucius said, "If that is all Father, I will go home and prepare for the journey."

"That is all, Son," his father said.

Lucius turned and left the anteroom. His spirits had been buoyed by the possible chance of promotion in the future. He would bide his time and hope his father performed well for the Emperor. Perhaps a well-placed word by his father at the appropriate time would be all it would take for Constantine to move him up the power structure also. He certainly hoped so. Lucius found himself smiling as he descended the steps of the Curia.

Maybe these political changes weren't so bad after all!

Chapter Twenty-five

It was the end of January and the weather had turned warm. For the last week the sun had shown and warmed the air and the earth. Even though Marcus knew that this was a week of false spring, he must go to the port and begin to make arrangements to go to Carthage. He asked his uncle if he could go to the port this morning and make the deliveries in the afternoon. He didn't want anyone else going to the Marius home but himself.

At the port, Marcus began to take an inventory of the vessels wintering there. Again, the only one going to Carthage was the Bonum Fortuna. The captain was inspecting his vessel and it looked like the repairs were finished. Marcus waited for him to finish and then asked permission to board the ship and speak to him.

"Sir," Marcus said, "I see you are still in port. Is your ship repaired and ready to sail?"

"Yes, when the sea opens, if the weather is good, I will sail. I follow the rule of 'Mare Clausum,' or closed sea. I do not set sail between the 12th of November and the 10th of March," the captain said.

"Do you still have a berth available for three persons?" Marcus asked.

"Yes, but if you wish one, you must pay part of the cost ahead of time," the captain answered.

"I thought that would be the case," Marcus said. He reached into the pouch he carried and gave the captain half of the cost for the journey. "We don't want to miss the ship, and with the weather turning so mild, I wanted to make sure when you might be sailing."

The captain smiled as he took the money. "Don't worry" he said, "if the weather holds, check with me on the 5th of March. I will give you our sailing date."

Marcus agreed and returned to the warehouse. He began making his deliveries and was nearing the Marius home. He rowed slowly to their dock. He must speak to Livia today, but it must be alone. He needed to talk to her and let her know what he was thinking. He wanted to talk of marriage, but it had to be done with the utmost secrecy. If any of the servants got a whiff of it, their plans would be compromised.

He knocked at the door and was greeted by one of the servants. "Master Marcus, I will tell Mistress Livia that you are here," he said.

Marcus unloaded the full barrels and was taking the empty ones back to the boat.

Livia came down the stairs and walked out to the boat to ask him in. "Not today," Marcus replied, "I am behind on my deliveries and can only stay a few minutes."

The look on her face told him she was disappointed. They were alone and no one was within hearing distance. "I went to the port this morning and made arrangements for our journey. I also wanted to make sure the captain was not planning to leave early because of the warm weather," he explained.

"It's all coming so quickly," Livia said.

Her face looked flushed and Marcus thought about if he should continue with what he wanted to talk to her about. He knew this might be the only chance he would have to speak to her alone. He stopped working and faced her directly. "Livia, we will be leaving within a month or so, and I need to talk to you about some things," he began. He started to speak the words he had been rehearsing in his mind for months. “We will be going to Carthage and I would like you to go as my wife. I know this is rather sudden, but I want you to take some time and think about it. My feelings have developed for you over the past several months, and there is nothing I want more than to be married to you for the rest of my life. If this is not what you want, I will still take you away from this home and watch over you in Carthage for as long as you wish.” There, he had said it, and he felt relief wash over him.

Livia was silent for a few moments before she spoke. “Marcus, she whispered, “I too, have been thinking of these things. I am not only committed to going, I am committed to going with you as your wife.”

Marcus’s heart leapt. “If I could, I would take you in my arms right now. As it is, we would betray ourselves if I even touched you. He turned away from her in order to control his emotions. He turned back and said, “Livia, I am so sorry for the years I was unkind to you. I felt that you had taken Stephanas away from me and I couldn’t forgive you for that.”

“I know,” she replied softly. He noticed tears were starting to form in her eyes.

“I also want you to know that even if all of this hadn’t happened, it was Father’s plan that we marry someday,” he went on.

“But why?” she asked.

“He promised Stephanas he would take care of you, and so he decided to leave you half of his estate and me the other half. The only way it would remain intact is if we would marry. He decided it the night of the funeral.”

She was silent for a moment as she pondered what he said. “So, is that what you were arguing about the next morning?” she asked.

"Yes, I didn't want him forcing me to do anything, especially marry the woman I had been angry at for the past five years." he explained.

Livia looked like she was trying to take it all in. Her face revealed her disappointment as she thought about what he had just said. "Marcus, I would never want you to marry me because your father asked you to," she said quietly.

"This had nothing to do with that," he answered quickly. "When I saw you here the first day, it was as if I was seeing you for the first time. I didn't see you as my brother's wife - I saw you as the woman you are. At first, I just wanted to take care of you and protect you from Lucius Marius. It was all that I could think of. Then, each time I saw you, my feelings deepened for you."

He saw relief wash over her face. "Do you really think we can make a life together in Carthage?" she whispered hesitantly.

She looked like the young girl his brother had married - shy and somewhat frightened.

Marcus's heart melted at her concerns. "I do Livia, I really do. I have done nothing but think and pray about it for months. I don't know what kind of a job I will get or what I will do to make a living, but I will do my best to support you and Rhea."

"I know you will, Marcus, and I want you to know that I trust you completely. We will leave in a few weeks together, and I trust that the Lord will make a way for us as we start our new life together."

She looked at him with longing. He could see the emotion on her face. She looked happy and yet frightened at the same time. "Leaving here will put so many people at risk," she said.

"I know," Marcus said gravely. "I think of it also, but it is what Father wants."

She stepped back as if trying to take it all in. He walked forward and was only inches from her. He could sense the emotion in her being as he was trying to control his own emotions. "I love you," he said hoarsely. "I was afraid that you wouldn't want to marry me after the way I treated you. I don't deserve you or your trust, but I am grateful to get both. I will hope that I can prove that to you."

Livia took another step back. She seemed afraid to be too close to him. "Marcus, I do love you; being near you makes me feel alive again. Sometimes I feel guilty because of my feelings for you."

A stab of sadness touched his heart as he thought of his brother. They had both lost so much when he left them. He felt right about this and he didn't feel like he was betraying his brother. He felt like he was doing exactly what his older brother would have wanted.

"This is right, Livia, I know it is. It is exactly what Stephanas would have wanted for both of us in this situation. I promise you that I will cherish your love and you will never be sorry you gave your love to me," he said.

He unlocked his gaze from hers and slowly turned to leave. "I must go now. We will be together soon, and nothing will ever separate us again."

"Until then," she said, as he pushed off from the dock.

He watched her as her silhouette became smaller and smaller. He looked at the house she was standing in front of. He was taking her away from a privileged life. He hoped he would be able to provide for her in the way he wanted. Doubts began to assail his mind, but he pushed them away. He loved her and he was determined to get her out of there, come what may.

Chapter Twenty-six

Lucius Marius stood in the court of the Emperor Constantine. He had been in Mediolanum these past few months, and he had been to the palace many times in order to speak with his father. As soon as they arrived, Constantine had allowed the senators to live at the palace. As official advisors, they had been housed and fed with the rest of the court advisors. To say his father was now close to the source of power was an understatement.

Last month, the Emperor Licinias had arrived from Illyria. He was one of two men who ruled the Roman Empire in the East. Constantine had arranged a marriage between his half-sister, Constantia, and Licinias. The marriage had taken place a few weeks ago and Lucius and his father had been invited to the ceremony. Never had one of their family been personally invited to a royal wedding; their fortunes were indeed rising.

Today, the 10th of March, they were all present at a special conference Constantine had called. They heard Constantine explain the particulars of the Edict the two Emperors had signed. The Edict would return all the property to the Church and to those individuals whose property had been seized during the last ten years of persecution. It made Christianity legal along with all other religions in the Empire. Many bishops had been asked to attend the conference and help work out the details as the Edict was enforced.

The Edict was read for all present to hear. Lucius looked around the room to gauge its impact on the faces of those present. As expected, his father's face was unreadable; he would not reveal his true feelings. There were many bishops of the church present, and they looked pleased beyond belief. Lucius kept his own face impassive; he was also skilled in the art of political intrigue. He could easily mask his inner feelings.

Men began to congratulate Constantine, and Lucius and his father were no exception. Lucius heard his father say, "Could there be anything better for the Empire? I think not." Lucius smiled and nodded in agreement. He did not want to be seen in any way disparaging the new law of the land. Besides, he knew that this Edict would change fortunes in the Empire for many years to come. He, for one, wanted to be on the winning side.

His father turned to him. "Lucius, walk with me."

Lucius looked surprised and began to keep in step with his father. His father continued. "Lucius, plans have changed. The Emperor wants a senator to go to Rome with a copy of the Edict and explain it to the full Senate. Even now the Senate is preparing statutes for municipalities in order to help with the legal transfer of properties."

"I can understand his thinking there," Lucius said. He was glad he was not the one going back to Rome. Mediolanum was where significant events were taking place.

"Who's going?"

"I am," his father said.

Lucius looked surprised, but said nothing.

"Your trip here has not been in vain. The Emperor is sending emissaries around the western part of the empire to make this new law known. I have asked him to send you to take a copy down the eastern side of Italia. You will meet with officials in each city and show them the document. They are to then announce it publicly. You must explain to them that the Emperor wants it enforced with all due haste."

Lucias smiled. He was now traveling at the pleasure of the Emperor. "I would be honored to serve him, Father." Lucius was indeed sincere when he spoke those words. He would have the Emperor's authority when he spoke and he liked the idea. In the past, he had traveled on behalf of the Senate, but Maxentius had gutted it of its power. Many of his trips these last several years had been a mere formality. This was indeed a new day for him. Nothing would please him more than to go.

"I thought you would feel that way," his father said and smiled.

"When do I leave?" Lucius asked.

"Within a few days. Constantine wants this Edict enforced as soon as possible," his father said.

"And when I am finished, do I return to Rome or to Mediolanum?" Lucius asked.

"I will be in Rome for a few months. Return there and then we will travel north together to Mediolanum. Constantine has decided it will be his capital for now and that is where we will be serving from. I will let the Senate know that you are now serving the Emperor as an emissary."

"When will the copies of the Edict be ready?" Lucius asked.

"In a few days all copies will be affixed with the Emperor's seal. That will be enough to convince any skeptic of their authenticity."

"I'll return in two days and shall leave as soon as they are ready," Lucius said.

He departed the palace in a good mood. Could the day have gone any better?

He would be leaving for the eastern half of Italia and would even be able to stop in Ravenna on his way south. He laughed to himself as he thought of Livia. He had given her months to recover from her loss and acquaint herself with his home. Now would be the time to get to know her better. He hoped to take her to his bed while he visited. Just the thought of her caused him to be aroused. He had thought little of women these past months. There was so much happening that he hadn't had time to pursue the matter. When he felt a physical need, he found one of the many attractive women servants at his home and satisfied it. He hoped to have more than a physical relationship with Livia. He hoped they could be friends. With this thought in mind, he returned home to pack for his journey.

Chapter Twenty-Seven

Livia sat at her dressing table. She looked in the mirror and saw the fatigue on her face. It had been a long day. Marcus had come in the morning to make his deliveries and had told her that tonight was the night. She had remained quiet and thoughtful all day. It saddened her to leave these people she had come to care about so deeply. She would especially miss Mago. He had taken her under his wing and taught her so much about running the house. He had cared for her as a daughter, but had treated her as an equal.

As much as she loved Junius, he had never taken her into his confidence as Mago had. He had allowed her to run the home, but he had kept the financial affairs of the household to himself. The many lessons Mago had taught her would be invaluable to her in the years to come.

She and Rhea had bathed earlier as they made their final preparations for their journey. Each of them would take a few tunics with them, a hairbrush and comb and that was it. They would not carry away more from this house than that. Marcus would be responsible to pack whatever else they would need for their journey. She hoped he would think about some of the things they may need on their trip.

As she passed the final hours in her room, she wrote Mago a letter of explanation.

She wanted to thank him, and she felt she owed him the truth of why she was leaving.

She sealed the letter with wax so that he would be the only one to read it. She carefully removed every stitch of clothing that she had on that she had not come with originally.

She would take nothing with her that she had been given. She had put the pearl necklace in the letter, so that there would be no question as to her integrity.

This was the second time in seven months that she was leaving the place she had called home. Before she left Junius's home, she had been able to say good-bye to each of the servants. How she wished she would have that opportunity again. She was surprised at the depth of feeling she had for each person in the Marius home. She had no desire to leave them, but she had every desire to leave Lucius Marius and his grasp on her.

As it neared midnight, she went into the next room to get Rhea. She was sitting on her bed awaiting their departure. "I guess it's time," Rhea said, as she saw Livia come in.

"Yes," Livia replied. "It's time." They took their sandals off and walked barefoot to the entrance. She opened the door and looked outside. She had been tempted to take an oil lamp to give them light as they went to the dock, but tonight the sky was clear and there was a full moon. Everything was bathed in a soft light. She closed the door and they walked around the house to the dock. She was relieved to see Marcus waiting for them.

"Livia, Rhea, thank God you're here!" Marcus said. He put their few belongings in the boat and helped them in. He then began to row away from the Marius home.

Livia turned back for a final look. The house was dark and no one had noticed their departure. She had worried so about their leaving. Could it really be this easy?

They remained silent as Marcus began to row. They all knew how sound carried on the water. Many nights they had heard men calling back and forth to each other as they rowed their boats on the canal in front of the house. Did they not know that everyone heard their voices?

Marcus had rowed for an hour or so and brought the boat up alongside a large dock. He secured the boat and then helped each one of them out in turn. He got their few belongings out and then turned and looked up on the road. He waved to Rufus who was waiting with the cart and Rufus steered the cart the final distance to the dock.

"Uncle Rufus," Livia started to say.

"Yes, child, it is I," he answered. "Let's get you loaded up and on your way." He took their belongings and put them in one of the trunks they would be bringing. "Marcus and I have tried to pack for your journey. We hope we put in much of what you will need.

I would have preferred that my wife had done this, but she has a tendency to talk too much and we couldn't risk your secret getting out."

Livia was relieved to see that they were taking more than the few things she and Rhea had secreted out of the house. Who knew what was in those two trunks, but anything had to be better than nothing at all. "Oh, thank you so much," she said, as she stifled the sob rising in her throat. She hugged him and did not want to let go.

"What is it, child?" he asked as he held her out at arm's length.

"I am so concerned for your family and for Junius and all those with him," she said.

"Don't you worry, we are all Roman citizens and as far as we can tell, no one has broken any laws. They can't arrest us for something we haven't done," he replied.

"But Lucius is so powerful! What will he do when he finds out we are gone?" she asked.

"Who knows when that will be?" Rufus said. "By the time he comes back, you could be in Carthage and it could all blow over quickly."

"I hope so," was all Liva could say. She doubted that it would all be that simple.

"Let's get all of you in the cart and be on our way. The ship is set to sail close to dawn." Rufus said.

They got on their way and began to travel towards the city gate. The gate would open soon and people would be coming in and out of the city. For a moment, Livia got nervous.What if someone recognized her? She then looked at her clothing and the cart.

She saw nothing out of the ordinary that would distinguish them in any way. They waited a while longer and the city gate was opened. The horses started moving forward and they left the city. No one paid any attention to them.

Once they were out of town a ways, Rufus pulled the cart aside. Marcus began, "Livia, since we have decided to marry, I wanted us to say our vows in front of Uncle Rufus and Rhea. They will be the witnesses of our commitment to each other.

Livia was stunned at the revelation, but as she thought about it for a few minutes, she could see the rightness of saying their vows now in front of the people they loved. She and Rhea stepped down from the cart and walked over in front of a large tree.

Everything seemed surreal to her as she faced Marcus.

Marcus took her hand and looked into her eyes. "I, Marcus Arvum, take you, Livia, to be my wife. I will love and care for you and be faithful to you as long as we both shall live. I take my vows in the name of the Father, Son and Holy Spirit." When he had finished saying that, he removed a tiny filigreed ring from his pocket. He took her hand and slipped it on her finger.

She looked at the ring and her eyes began to fill with tears. She fought for control of her emotions and then she took Marcus's hand. She began, "I, Livia Arvum, take you, Marcus, to be my husband. I will serve you, love and care for you, and be faithful to you as long as we both shall live. I take these vows in the name of the Father, the Son and the Holy Spirit."

Marcus took her in his arms and kissed her briefly. She felt his lips on hers and the strength of his arms around her. She was comforted by the power of his touch. She was aware of Rhea and Rufus and did not let her emotions and body go in the direction they wanted to.

She turned to Rufus and Rhea and said, "Thank you so much for witnessing our vows. I truly feel we are married and I can depart in peace knowing you both shared these precious moments with us."

They all got back into the cart and continued on the road to Classis. It was just beginning to get light as they entered the port city. Rufus knew his way around as he had picked up hundreds of orders at the docks. He drove the cart to the dock in front of the ship. He stopped and took some bread, cheese and water out of the bag at his feet.

"Here, have something to eat before you get on board," he said as he handed each one something to eat. They ate quietly and sat there until the sun began to rise.

"After I get you safely on the ship, I will ride out and let Junius know that you are on your way to freedom," he said.

"Thank you," Marcus replied. "Father will be pleased to know that we have gotten away."

As it began to get light, they could see the Bonum Fortuna come to life. The captain was shouting orders to one sailor and then to another as he readied the ship to sail.

Marcus got out of the cart and felt a sudden gust of wind. He looked behind him to the west and the dark clouds were almost on top of them. He felt a drop or two of moisture. He turned and walked up the gangplank in order to let the captain know of their arrival.

The captain told him to bring the women on board as they would be departing soon.

As he walked down the gangplank, the wind continued to pick up. He knew the storm would be upon them soon. He hurried back to the cart in order to get the women on the ship before the rain hit.

"Let's go," he said and helped Livia and Rhea down from the cart. Rufus stepped down also to bid them all good-bye. Livia hugged him again and turned to go. She and Rhea followed Marcus up the gangplank. They met the captain and were shown to their quarters.

It had seriously begun to rain as Marcus returned to the cart. He and Rufus carried each trunk on board and stowed them in their cabin. Rufus turned again to them and said, "May God go with you my children." His eyes began to water at the thought of the possibility that he might not see them again. He turned to go so that they would not see the emotion he was struggling to contain.

By the time he reached his cart, the sky had opened up in earnest. He sought shelter under a large tree to wait out the storm. He didn't want to return to Caesarea in the pouring rain. He watched the ship from his temporary shelter. It was still at anchor and was not moving. He would not feel relieved until the ship actually left the harbor.

Marcus, Livia and Rhea sat in their cabin and listened as the rain pelted the ship. It had been at least an hour and there had been no let up. The ship had not left the harbor and Marcus decided to go ask the captain when they would be leaving.

"It's bad luck to leave in the middle of a storm. I have waited here all winter for fair weather, and I won't leave until this squall abates," he said. "Why are you so anxious to leave? We'll be on our way soon enough."

Marcus did not answer the captain's question and glumly returned to the cabin. "We can't depart until the storm's over," he reported to the women. "I won't feel safe until we are on our way," he continued.

Livia tried to think of some words that would console Marcus, but she felt the exact same way. Until they were actually out to sea, she would not feel like they had truly gotten away from Lucius Marius. She looked at Rhea, and could see that she was feeling the same way. It was hard to disguise the fear that was in each of their eyes.

"Mago will have read the letter by now. I don't know if he will try to look for us or not. If he does, he will come looking for you, Marcus, at the warehouse," she said.

"No one knows anything there. Uncle Rufus and I have not told anyone about our plans. The men working there will not be lying to him when they say they don't know where I am," Marcus replied.

They sat there silently while the rain continued on unabated for another few hours.

Finally, about midmorning, the rain stopped. The clouds began to clear and the sun came out. They all walked out of the cabin and went on deck as the captain gave the order to weigh anchor. They watched as the sails caught the wind and the ship began to turn and face the open sea.

They moved to the back of the ship and watched the land slowly recede from the horizon. Fatigue suddenly descended on Livia. "I'm going to go lay down," she said.

"Me, too," Rhea replied.

"I want to stay on deck a while longer," Marcus said.

The women returned to their berth and laid down. They were both fast asleep when Marcus returned to the cabin. Marcus got in the bed as quietly as he could in order not to disturb Livia. Her back was to him, and he lay down. He placed his arm around her waist and relished the nearness of her. He had waited months and now he was finally able to touch the woman he loved.

Livia awoke with a start. There was someone in her bed. As she took in her surroundings, she remembered where she was. She turned and faced Marcus. He was smiling and staring at her with his dark eyes. She opened her mouth to say something and he placed his finger over it to silence her.

He looked over to where Rhea was sleeping. She was snoring loudly and looked like she could sleep through anything. Livia looked over at her and nodded to him and smiled. He kissed her deeply, and she returned the kiss. He slowly began to caress her body and she responded to his touch. Her emotions began to rise and she felt a hunger for him. Eagerly, she surrendered her body to his, and soon the marriage had been consummated.

Afterwards they just stared into each other's eyes. Marcus kissed her face softly and quietly expressed his love for her. Livia felt truly happy for the first time in months. She wanted to stay awake, but the gentle rocking of the ship was putting her to sleep. She tried to keep her eyes open, but couldn't. Finally, she lay her head in the crook of his arm and gave in to her exhaustion. She fell asleep, feeling secure in his love.

Chapter Twenty-Eight

Lucius Marius stood on the veranda of the inn. He and his soldiers had slept there the night before. They had been traveling from Verona and had arrived there late last evening. They were only about thirty miles from Ravenna and he was anxious to get home. They had awoken to a downpour and had eaten breakfast, hoping it would end soon. Unfortunately, it had continued until mid-morning.

The clouds were breaking up and the sky was clearing. He mounted his chariot and soon they were on their way. He looked around and smelled the ocean air. He had always loved this coastal region and the thought of being home soon buoyed his spirits.

He looked out over the Adriatic when the view afforded itself. He even thought he had seen a ship far out in the distance. If he did, it was a good sign that spring had finally come to the region.

Lucius was anxious to be home. He had been looking forward to this time ever since he left in the fall. He wanted to spend time with Livia; getting to know her, and cementing their relationship. He was sure she would be over much of her grief, and she would be ready to start a relationship with him. He was hoping they would be able to consummate their friendship in his bedroom within a few days. That is what he had really been looking forward to all winter. There was something so attractive about this woman that he had been willing to wait for her and not press his advantage too soon.

It was mid-afternoon when they finally arrived at the house. Mago greeted him with a sense of surprise as he usually did when he had been gone for any length of time.

"I'll take a bath, and then would you please prepare a meal for my men and me; we are famished from our journey," Lucius said.

Mago ordered the bath prepared and went to the kitchen to see how the preparations for the evening meal were going. He had the women fix a light meal for Lucius and his men. He knew very soon he was going to have to tell the master that Livia was gone. He would wait until his master was bathed and dressed and then he would tell him the news. There was going to be a maelstrom and he was not looking forward to it.

Mago slowly went up the stairs to the third floor. He had seen his master angry before, and he knew he would not react well to the news that was coming. He approached the master's bedroom. Iris had helped the master dress and was arranging his hair. He waited until Iris was finished and then he dismissed her.

"Master Lucius, I need to tell you of an unfortunate incident that happened this morning," Mago began.

Lucius looked up inquisitively. He had rarely seen his servant so morose; this was not going to be good news. "Proceed," was all he said.

"This morning Livia and Rhea were not at breakfast. I assumed there was a problem and went to find Iris as she usually helped Livia get ready in the morning. I found Iris in Livia's room crying. "What is wrong?" I asked her. "The mistress is gone, and her servant, too. I was afraid to come and tell you," she said.

I looked around the room and she was right. All of the clothes and shoes we purchased for her were neatly arranged in the closet. The bed was made and so was the one in her servant, Rhea's room. They were nowhere to be found in the house.

"By the gods," Lucius muttered. "If any of you has caused her harm or made her unhappy, you will be flogged within an inch of your lives. I gave strict instructions to do everything you could to make her welcome in my home."

Mago was silent for a few moments. He had never lied to his master and he wasn't about to start now, especially since their lives would be worthless in his sight until he knew the truth. He hated to betray Livia's trust, but for the good of the household he would share what he knew. "She left a letter for me on her dressing table," was all he said as he handed Lucius the letter.

Mago,

I truly want to thank you for the kindness you have shown me ever since I arrived here. I could not have asked for more consideration than what I have been shown. Each servant went out of their way to be helpful to me in my new role in this home. I have grown to care for each of you deeply, and I can honestly say that I could have stayed here for the rest of my life, if it hadn't been for one thing. I cannot be more to your Master than just a servant. I know he wants more from me, but my conscience will not allow me to share my body or my bed with him. I am a Christian, first and foremost, and I will not betray my Lord.

Livia

Lucius sat there silently stunned for a few minutes. "A Christian," he spat out, "in my own home?" It was not a question, nor did he expect an answer. The bile began to form in his stomach and he could almost taste it in his mouth.

"What have you done to look for her?" Lucius asked, eyeing him warily. He felt himself getting angrier by the moment. Had Mago been part of this betrayal? He dismissed the thought, knowing it was not true.

Mago could see his master's face getting redder and redder. He could feel the tension in the air. His master was not yelling and this was a bad sign. He was very, very quiet and Mago knew that meant that his master was beyond angry; he was livid. He could see the murderous intent in his eyes.

"I sent a servant out to her father-in-law's and no one had seen her or knew she was gone. I sent another servant to inquire of her at the wine dealer's, and no one had seen her or her brother for that matter," Mago stated.

"She doesn't have a brother, you imbecile," Lucius yelled.

Mago had rarely seen his master so angry. He remembered back to when Livia had first introduced him to Marcus. He could see her face as she introduced Marcus. She had not finished talking when he had welcomed Marcus. "Perhaps, she was about to say brother-in-law?" he thought to himself. "I have not known where else to look," Mago said honestly.

Lucius began to think out loud. "She wouldn't go to her father-in-law's. That is the first place we would look. She wouldn't go anywhere obvious. Does she think I cannot find her? She wasn't on the road going north or we would have intercepted her. What about south, could she have gone south or was she hiding with someone she knew in Ravenna?"

"She never mentioned knowing anyone in Ravenna other than the young man named Marcus," Mago said. "He works for Rufus, the wine dealer."

"Leave me alone and let me think," Lucius said. "I will be down shortly to eat."

Mago excused himself. This was not going to be good. Lucius was a master at intrigue and deceit. If anyone could figure out where she had gone, it would be Lucius. Mago went to the kitchen to make sure the food would be ready to serve when the master came down. The other servants eyed him warily. They had been as disappointed and sad as he had been this morning when they had discovered her gone. A few had even cried like Iris had done.

"The master is in a foul mood. Be very careful to do everything exactly as you are supposed to this evening. He will not tolerate ineptness tonight," Mago warned them.

Lucius came down and ate his meal in silence. He was frustrated at how close he had been to seeing her. He had only missed her by a few hours. He swore to himself that he would have her if it was the last thing he did. No one crossed Lucius Marius and went unscathed when he caught up to them. There were a hundred places she could go and hide from him. But where, which way did she go?

Mago stood in the room as his master ate. He felt bad for Livia. He knew his master would not be kind if he caught up to her. He began to dislike his master in a way he never had before. Livia had been kind to all of them and had served his master well. He did not want anything bad to happen to her.

Lucius continued to ruminate on the problem. He wanted to find the girl and bring her back. He would have to be quick about it or her trail would go cold within a few days.

The thought of losing her made him sick inside; he had looked forward to partaking of her delights all winter. He left the table and returned to the third floor for the evening.

The next morning Lucius came down for breakfast in a better mood. He was sure he would be able to find out something about her. He called Gaius to the table. "You remember where the girl lived?"

"Of course, Sire," Gaius replied, "we spent several days there."

"I want you to go and ask her father-in-law again if he has seen her or knows where she is. I might be wrong about it; she could have gone there and is in hiding. You will know if he is lying. Report back to me as soon as you return," Lucius said.

He looked to Mago. "You, take one of the soldiers and return to the wine dealer. Take some money, also, and see if you can bribe anyone around there. Someone must know something; they just couldn't vanish into thin air."

Mago turned to leave. "And Mago, when you are finished at the wine dealer's, continue on south to Classis and see if you can get any information out of anyone at the docks. Someone is bound to have some information somewhere."

Mago and the young soldier left immediately for the wine dealer's in the Caesarea district. He had been there several times, but he dreaded this particular visit. He entered the warehouse and saw Rufus working there as usual. Rufus looked up at Mago, and then looked away quickly, guilt written all over his face.

Rufus took a deep breath and turned towards him, "Mago, what can I help you with?"

Mago studied him for a moment. He looked around the warehouse. There were others working there and he didn't want everyone to know the reason for his errand. He decided to veil his words. “My master has lost something valuable and he wanted to know if you have seen it or know where it could be.”

Rufus replied truthfully, “I don’t know where it is,” and he didn’t. The ship could be anywhere.

“Then, you are aware, something is missing?” Mago asked again.

“Yes,” Rufus answered truthfully again, “I am missing something myself.”

“My master is anxious to have it returned to him,” Mago said.

“I wasn’t aware that your master owned it,” Rufus replied, a little too harshly.

“He doesn’t. It was on loan to him and he is concerned about the welfare of it. My master will go to any lengths and pay any price to retrieve it.” Mago stated candidly.

“I cannot tell him where it is,” Rufus said with finality.

Mago knew that he was not going to get any information out of him, and turned to leave. He turned one more time and said to Rufus reluctantly, “Unfortunately, we will not be able to do business with this establishment anymore.”

Rufus was not surprised by the statement. He had been expecting it. “I’m sorry that we will not be able to serve you any longer.”

Mago and the soldier left and continued on to the port at Classis. There were a few ships in port and Mago wondered if Livia, Rhea and Marcus could be on one of them.

It was about noon when they arrived and the docks were quiet. Men were sitting around in small groups eating what they had carried to work with them. Mago approached one of the groups of men. “Excuse me, some of our hired help has gone missing, and I was wondering if any of you has seen them?” Margo queried.

“Did they steal anything?” a surly worker asked belligerently.

“No, they were extremely valuable, and my master hates to lose them. One was a young woman with dark hair and one an older woman in her thirties. They would have been accompanied by a young man with dark hair,” Mago explained. The men looked at each other, as if deciding whether to talk to the strangers or not.

“My master will make it worth your while if you have any information for him,” Mago continued. He took the money pouch out and let it jingle in the men’s ears.

“There was a young couple with an older lady that got on the boat yesterday,” the youngest of them said.

Mago hesitated; he didn’t want to know this information but knew he must query further because of the soldier standing by. “And which of these boats would that be?” he asked, knowing he was about to betray Livia.

The young man replied, “Neither, sir. It was the boat that left yesterday. It was headed for Carthage.”

“So, perhaps they did get away,” Mago thought to himself and smiled inwardly.

He reached into the coin purse and brought out a few denarii. He held it in front of the man. “Thank you, young man, you have been most helpful.”

Mago turned and walked away quickly. There was nothing more they could do. They would report the turn of events to Lucius and hope he would forget about her in due time.

“Come on,” he said to the soldier as they left the dock area. “We’ve gotten all of the information we need.”

They returned home and Mago found Lucius in the library. Lucius looked up at him and wanted to know what he had found out. "A dock worker said he saw some people resembling their description board a ship yesterday. It was heading for Carthage," Mago stated calmly. He watched Lucius' face carefully. His lips tightened in a straight line and his eyes narrowed.

"Do you think it was them?" he asked.

"It could have been, it could have been someone else, I don't know. The ship had already left, so I could ask no further," Mago said.

"You may go. I will wait to hear what Gaius finds out." Lucius replied.

Mago left feeling uneasy. His master was furious and would not be bested easily by the runaways.

Gaius returned without any information. If Junius did know where they were, he wasn't telling. Lucius was not surprised; he hadn't really expected much from Junius. Lucius spent the afternoon in thought. He had his spies everywhere. He knew people in Carthage who could be on the lookout for her. He would send a message that she had stolen something very rare from him and that she and her accomplices should be arrested on arrival. He would get the authorities involved and she would not be safe from him there.

He carefully penned out a message and went to the cages where he kept his homing pigeons. He fastened the message to a bird's leg and released it. It rose in the air, circled and then began to fly in a southerly direction.

Satisfied, Lucius watched it until it was a small speck in the sky. He smiled grimly. "I can hardly wait for her to arrive in Carthage to my little welcoming party," he thought to himself. He was going to make this woman and her friends pay for what they had done to him. He turned and walked back into his house.

Mago watched his master from behind the curtains. He could only guess what he had just done. He saw the homing pigeon fly south, also. For the first time in his life, Mago wanted to circumvent his master's plans. But how, what could he do? His family had come from Carthage a few generations ago, he was even named after the brother of the Carthaginian general, Hannibal. He did not know any one there now, and he had no way to contact anyone. He stood there staring at his master, the frustration mounting inside of him. A thought came unbidden into his mind, but he dismissed it. It came again. He felt uncomfortable but he would do it. He closed his eyes momentarily and prayed to the Christian god, whoever he was, "Please watch over them, wherever they are, and protect them from Master Lucius."

Mago suddenly felt a peace come over him. Perhaps this god could answer prayers. Perhaps he could watch over Livia, Marcus and Rhea wherever they were. He certainly hoped so.

Made in the USA
Columbia, SC
25 August 2022

66087178R00100